TUNBRIDGE AND SCOTTISH SOUVENIR WOODWARE

ALSO BY EDWARD H. PINTO, F.S.A.

The Craftsman in Wood
Treen and Other Wooden Bygones

1. (*upper*): Two fine Tunbridge early geometric pattern trays, a cube pattern paper weight and a cube and vandyke pattern bottle case, all *circa* 1830. Also a fine, tambour enclosed inkstand, *circa* 1865, by Barton. The interior of the inkstand is shown in Plate 3. Bottle case and paper weight in the private collection of the authors; the other examples, *Pinto Collection, Birmingham Museum.*

2. (*lower*): Pencil and pen box, reel box with lid on left, silk-skein holder, pair of reticule frames, needle book and stickware box, all in Tunbridge mosaic *circa* 1845–50. On the right, nineteenth-century Sorrento mosaic photograph frame and octagonal casket, and twentieth-century 'mule' paper knife. The reel box, reticule frames and Sorrento mosaic, *Pinto Collection, Birmingham Museum*; the other items in the private collection of the authors.

TUNBRIDGE AND SCOTTISH SOUVENIR WOODWARE

WITH CHAPTERS ON
BOIS DURCI AND PYROGRAPHY

EDWARD & EVA PINTO

LONDON
G. BELL & SONS
1970

PRINTED IN GREAT BRITAIN BY
BUTLER & TANNER LTD, FROME AND LONDON

ISBN 0 7135 1772 7

To Lord David Stuart

whose generosity in placing the results of his research at our disposal has added greatly to the completeness of the Scottish souvenir woodware section of this book.

Contents

Illustrations

Plates

Figures

Acknowledgments

OUR ESPECIAL thanks are due to Lord David Stuart for most generously placing at our disposal the full fruits of his intensive research on Scottish woodware, spread over more than twenty years and also to the Marquess of Bute for making available to us unpublished material from his family archives. Both Lord David Stuart and we ourselves are considerably indebted to Mr. Stuart Maxwell of the National Museum of Antiquities of Scotland, for much important information. Mr. R. G. Sandbach of Tunbridge Wells Museum has been correspondingly helpful in aiding our research on Tunbridge products.

In addition, we offer our thanks to all the following, who have either volunteered interesting information or have patiently answered our questions in connection with:

1. *Tunbridge Ware and Tunbridge Wood Mosaic:* Miss Sylvia Groves; Mr. A. Frank Hemsley; Mr. M. Howard; Mr. G. Bernard Hughes; Mrs. Therle Hughes; Mr. David Kent; Mr. C. W. Musgrave, Director, Brighton Pavilion; Mrs. C. H. Watkins (USA).

2. *Scottish Souvenir Woodware:* Miss C. Armet, archivist to the Marquess of Bute; Mr. R. Blane, *Ayr Advertiser*; Mrs. D. C. Bowser; Mrs. H. Browne; Mr. John Buist; Mrs. E. D. Campbell; Mrs. G. Chalmers; Mr. I. W. Dunlop; Mr. T. Findlay; Mr. Ian Finlay, Royal Scottish Museum; Mr. Douglas Fraser; Mr. Edwin R. Freeston; Mr. T. Gray, County Archivist, Carlisle; Mr. John Hair, County Clerk, Ayr; Mr. John C. Hay; Mr. E. Austin Hinton, City Librarian, Newcastle-upon-Tyne; Group Captain P. W. Lowe Holmes; Miss J. D. Hyslop; Mr. Peter Klein, Birmingham Museum; Mr. Herbert B. Lang; Mr. S. G. Layton; Mr. J. McCaig, formerly County Clerk, Ayr; Mr. B. R. S. Megaw, formerly of the Manx Museum; Mr. D. C. Mitchell;

Miss Mary Muir; Miss M. Reid; John Sellers Ltd.; William Sessions Ltd.; 'Solway II' of the *Cumberland News*; Mr. W. G. Stanley; Mrs. Y. Stewart (S. Africa); Mr. B. L. Thompson; Mr. Timothy Trace (USA); Miss L. Walsh; Mrs. E. H. W. Williamson: Mr. A. F. Wilson, Ayr C.C.; Miss Y. M. Wilson; Mr. V. H. Woods, Birmingham Reference Library.

The illustration of the games table at Kensington Palace is reproduced by gracious permission of H.M. The Queen. For permission to reproduce photographs of specimens in their collections our grateful thanks are also tendered to the Marquess of Bute, Lord David Stuart, Lord Faringdon, The Royal Botanic Gardens, Kew, Birmingham Museum and Art Gallery, and Tunbridge Wells Museum.

We also wish to acknowledge to the following our indebtedness for permission to reproduce extracts from articles, by one or both of us, which have appeared in *Apollo*, *British Plastics*, *Country Life*, *Cumberland News*, *The Scotsman*, *The Times*, *The Woodworker*.

Finally, in the production of this book we would like to thank our publishers, Messrs. G. Bell & Sons, for their usual full co-operation and particularly their director, Mr. S. L. Dennis, for his unsparing personal interest and helpful guidance.

Introduction

THIS book describes four entirely different nineteenth-century productions—Tunbridge wood mosaic ware, Scottish pen-and-ink, tartan and transfer ware, *Bois Durci*, and pyrography. The first two cover many of the same range of objects and have the additional relationship that much of the range was designed to form useful souvenirs of places visited. *Bois Durci* was a completely new material, a wood-based plastic invented by a Frenchman and intended for moulding useful and decorative objects, some of them souvenirs of events, at much lower cost than was possible by hand work. Pyrography, which had earlier ancestry, was, in the nineteenth century, almost if not entirely a non-commercial hobby craft.

As regards souvenirs, one may well wonder why there is such a large and attractive selection of nineteenth-century ware available for collecting, but virtually none of earlier date. The first solution which may spring to mind is the Industrial Revolution—the advent of machinery, steam power, gas engines and, before the century ended, electric power. Even if this were the correct answer, and in the case of ornamental woodware it is not, it would only be one half, and the less important half of the story, because supply and demand are closely intermixed.

Before examining why demand was so limited in earlier times, let us consider the true effects of industrialization on the making of woodware. The short answer is that the effect on making was practically nil: when the makers of Tunbridge wood mosaic and the Scottish wood craftsmen established their workshops during the first quarter of the nineteenth century, the making of the various objects was already as mechanized as it was ever to become, but there was a large element of hand labour. The technique of Tunbridge wood mosaic was and always remained largely a hand craft. As time went on, the Scots endeavoured to meet increasing competition from other materials which lent themselves better to mechanization, by changing from hand *decoration* of their ware to other types of ornament which lent themselves to mechanical reproduction. Although the wages of men and women fluctuated during the century according to supply and demand, there was overall a considerable rise. Tunbridge and Scottish woodware were always of good quality and expensive in their day. Although competition forced down prices, neither the Kentishmen nor the Scots would tolerate shoddy products; so the high element of hand labour and decreasing profit margins eventually forced the makers of souvenir woodware to succumb to the competition of pressed and die stamped metal objects, moulded plastics, and woven souvenirs, such as Stevengraphs. In fact, the Industrial Revolution, far from proving beneficial, eventually killed the manufacture of the woodware, which could not keep pace with the newer techniques. Turnery was probably the last of the woodware to go, because the lathe, the origins of which are lost in antiquity, turns out work complete and at low cost; but the various rectangular boxes and other related objects all entailed hand assembly and finishing, even though mechanical saws, planes and drills were used in the preparatory stages. Mechanical drills and saws had been used at least as early as the seventeenth century, but it is not sufficiently well known that as early as 1791, Sir Samuel Bentham set up the first factory for making a range of planing, moulding, rebating, grooving and sawing machines. In 1793, he obtained an inclusive patent, No. 1838, which covered the basic elements of nearly every modern woodworking machine.

There are a number of fundamental factors to account for the vast increase in demand for woodware and other manufactures as souvenirs during the nineteenth century. The population of England, Scotland and Wales, which was under 12 millions in 1801, had become 21 millions by 1851 and 37 millions in 1901. The increase and speed-up in travel facilities were sensational. At the beginning of the century, the alternatives were still the same as in Roman times—on foot, horseback, or in horse-drawn vehicles. When Victoria came to the throne, there were just over 500 miles of railway track; only a decade later, there were some 5,000 miles. Before long, the bicycle, tricycle and pedal goods vehicle were adding mobility, whilst on the seas, traffic was being revolutionized by the change from sail to steam. These developments greatly increased home and international business travel, transport of goods, and journeys for pleasure. A further result of the foregoing was that many more people than ever before went out to work, and because of the excess of females over males, many more women and girls became wage earners in domestic service, shops, and workshops or factories. The emancipation of women had begun and there was thus an improvement in the standard of living of an increasing proportion of the population; nevertheless, there were, throughout the century, much grinding poverty and severe hardship.

Whilst working conditions and hours of labour were both generally appalling by modern standards, they improved gradually, leading by degrees to a little leisure and a small amount of pleasure spending money for manual workers of both sexes, and more of both for the middle classes. At first the journeys of this new class of travellers were largely met by cheap day trips; later, week or longer holidays became more common and the whole family participated. Although holidays with pay were rare throughout the century, quite early in the industrial era, industries in certain areas closed down for holidays at regular times, such as the Lancashire cotton Wakes Week, the Yorkshire woollen Bowlingtide holidays and the Glasgow annual Fair holidays. Until the nineteenth century, holidays away from home had, with few exceptions, been the prerogative of the wealthy, and had consisted largely of the grand tour of Europe, mostly for gentlemen only, or visits to the English spas, ostensibly to recover from the effects of over-indulgence. Actually, however, these were fashionable pilgrimages at more or less fixed times of the year, with considerable gaiety to counteract the ritual of 'taking the waters' and probably with sufficient rich food, drink and late nights to nullify any beneficent effects there might have been from the cure. The new nineteenth-century holiday makers wanted something quite different and the story of souvenirs is, therefore, tied up, to a great extent, with the new types of seaside resorts which sprang up to meet the new demand.

Seaside resorts were not all new at the beginning of the nineteenth century, but the number was very limited, and they were largely 'cures' for the wealthy—merely alternatives to the innumerable 'spaws' inland, which the intrepid horsewoman and spa addict, Celia Fiennes, had visited and reported in her diary during the late seventeenth century.

Sea bathing took a long time to obtain medical acceptance and the further advancement to that of a pleasurable pastime and exercise was inordinately slow. Dr. John Wittie, in his book *Scarborough Spa*, extolled the virtues of sea bathing for gout, in 1667. The spa's waters (visited by the redoubtable Celia in 1697) had long been famous, but the town's development as the first English sea bathing resort only dates from the 1730s. Early seaside resorts followed the social pattern of inland spas, with masters of ceremonies, assembly rooms, libraries, sometimes a theatre, and a constant round of balls, concerts and lectures. In 1749, Dr. Richard Russell, a Brighthelmstone (Brighton) physician, published *Dissertation on the Use of Sea Water*, in Latin. Translated into English in 1752, it helped considerably in popularizing 'dipping' or sea bathing, although how many found benefit from drinking sea-water, as Dr. Russell advocated, is unknown.

George III's numerous visits to Weymouth and his son's even more numerous visits to, and sojourns at, Brighthelmstone in the late eighteenth century, greatly helped the seaside holiday cult. Although the Prince Regent was a greater influence than the railways in transforming the Sussex fishing village of Brighthelmstone into the fashionable resort of Brighton, it was the railways which converted it from a Court annex to a popular holiday resort.

The eighteenth century's addition of the seaside, to spas, as a place for the wealthy to go, was summed up by William Cowper, in 1782, in his poem *Retirement*—

> *Your prudent grandmammas, ye modern belles,*
> *Content with Bristol, Bath and Tunbridge Wells,*
> *When health required it would consent to roam,*
> *Else more attached to pleasures found at home.*
> *But now alike, gay widow, virgin, wife,*
> *Ingenious to diversify dull life,*
> *In coaches, chaises, caravans and hoys,*
> *Fly to the coast for daily, nightly joys,*
> *And all, impatient of dry land, agree*
> *With one consent to rush into the sea.*

The popularity of inland spas was, with few exceptions, unaffected by the growth of seaside resorts during the nineteenth century. The ancient Tunbridge Wells had one of its greatest periods of prosperity during the nineteenth century, helped by the fame of its fashionable promenade, The Pantiles, and its specialized craft of wood mosaic. Bath, *Aquae Sulis* of the

Romans, with its 500,000 gallons a day hot spring, emerging at 120° Fahrenheit, retained its long-established pre-eminence. Although it gave its name to Bath chairs and Bath buns, curiously, it never developed a distinctive local souvenir trade, although noted for its luxury shops. Probably this was because its habitués, mostly of considerable wealth, already had so much, particularly in the way of works of art—souvenirs of their youthful grand tours of Europe. In the nineteenth century, Leamington, Cheltenham, Droitwich, Harrogate, Clifton, Llandrindod Wells, Woodhall Spa, Strathpeffer, and so on, reached new heights of prosperity. Most of the spas which went downhill, such as Epsom, patronized by Nell Gwynn, did so either from lack of enterprise, or because expansion of housing or commerce in their vicinity blotted out the actual springs, or destroyed their amenities and relaxation values. The final blows, from which many of the spas never recovered, were the travel and other restrictions of World War II, and the after-effects, including the National Health Act. Spas were included within that service and, at the time of writing, only eight are sufficiently large to be fully operational, but as time goes on, the treatment facilities are gradually being built into local hospitals and the spa character of some of these centres is changing.

The history of both the Scottish and the Tunbridge souvenir woodware is not only tied up, to a great extent, with British spas but, as our story will tell, both industries owe something to Spa (now in Belgium), which gave its name to all health resorts with curative spring waters.

How the various local industries associated with spas, like Whitby and Scarborough jet, were gradually superseded by goods manufactured in specialized centres further afield, is also told in the pages of this book. So also are the reasons for the eventual decay of the manufacturing centres which, additional to supplying souvenirs to spas, also catered for the growing towns patronized by the new classes of holiday makers.

This book has no bibliography because, so far as we know, there are no earlier books devoted to any of the subjects it covers; but a number of articles, including several by us, have appeared from time to time, concerning Scottish and Tunbridge products, *Bois Durci*, and pyrography. Over the years, a number of misapprehensions have crept in concerning the origins and history of the first two types of manufacture; these have proliferated, owing to later writers repeating the errors of earlier ones. We have, therefore, ignored as far as possible articles written during the last hundred years, concerning the origins of those industries which go back a further half century, and we have gone back with our research, as far as we have been able, to contemporary records of events.

We had some extremely good luck in our investigations on Scottish ware, and an account of the somewhat remarkable coincidences which occurred during our research is included in Part II, *The Smiths of Mauchline and their Contemporaries.*

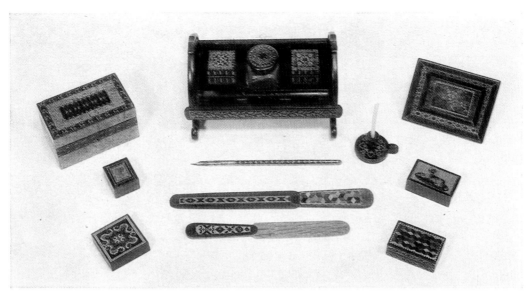

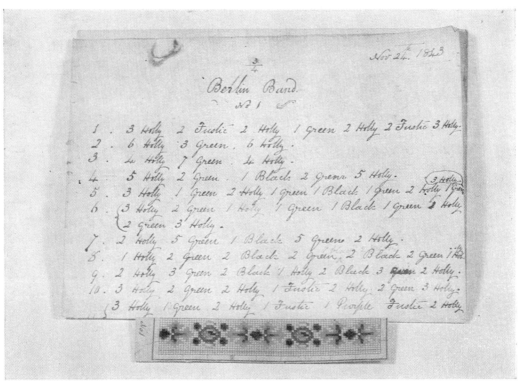

3. Interior of the Barton tambour inkstand shown closed in Plate 1 and left, *circa* 1830 bird's-eye maple box. The pin tray, pen holder, paper knives, taper holder, stamp box, etc., *circa* 1845. All items except the tambour inkstand, in the private collection of the authors.

4. A Fenner & Nye manuscript assembly chart dated 1843, together with coloured pattern for a ¾-in. 'Berlin woolwork' banding, painted on graph paper. *Pinto Collection, Birmingham Museum.*

PART ONE

TUNBRIDGE WARE &
TUNBRIDGE WOOD MOSAIC

CHAPTER ONE

Tunbridge Ware before Mosaic

THE TERM Tunbridge ware has been used to describe a changing range of products of entirely different appearance during the seventeenth, eighteenth and nineteenth centuries. From the point of view of the historian bent on research, this use of the same word for differently finished or decorated wares, made over such a long period, is most unfortunate because it often makes it impossible to state, with absolute certainty, exactly when the various changes of fashion took place. It is particularly unlucky that no contemporary recorded at the time, or that no absolutely contemporary record survived, as to who invented, or when or where the ingenious block or end grain mosaic was invented, which brought fresh fame to Tunbridge Wells in the nineteenth century; what we have been able to elicit about these problems will be found in Chapters 2 and 3.

The position is complicated today because most dealers, and the collectors of Tunbridge wood mosaic, whose number is increasing rapidly, do not know of the earlier wares and, therefore, describe the mosaic as Tunbridge ware. That the mosaic is being collected so widely is understandable, for although prices have risen considerably during the last twenty years, it is still possible to obtain it at reasonable prices, it is highly decorative and is available in an extremely wide range of useful objects. This chapter of the book tells briefly the history of the earlier wares, whilst the two chapters which follow set out points of particular interest to collectors of the fascinating nineteenth-century wood mosaic.

Tonbridge, sometimes in the past spelt Tunbridge (as in Fig. 1, Chapter 2), goes back to Norman England and its name, incorporating 'tun' or cask, suggests that it was an early centre of coopering. This is likely, because the neighbourhood is still well wooded, but formerly it provided such a wide selection of English timber that it was not surprising that a flourishing and specialized industry in turnery and small cabinet ware grew up in the vicinity. Tonbridge was a sizeable town before neighbouring Tunbridge Wells even developed into a village in the seventeenth century, following Lord North's discovery of the chalybeate springs in 1606. The Wells soon acquired a reputation for its waters, as a fashionable summer resort and as a healthy place of escape from the various plagues which ravaged insanitary London.

Tunbridge Wells did not acquire its prefix 'Royal' until the reign of Edward VII, but according to that reliable and most interesting historian Thomas Benge Burr, who wrote *The History of Tunbridge Wells* in 1766, Queen Henrietta Maria, wife of Charles I, was the first royalty to visit the Wells. She came for her health on May 29, 1630, following the birth of Charles II. She stayed about six weeks and owing to the then shortage of accommodation, she and her entourage dwelt in tents all the time, their camp being pitched on Bishop's-Down-Common at the top of Mount Ephraim.

According to Benge Burr, there was not much accommodation for visitors until the period 1670–90, when a considerable building of lodgings took place. However, John Evelyn found a cottage to suit him in June 1652, when he recorded in his *Diary*:

> 'My Wife being discompos'd by having been so long at sea, we set not forth towards home until ye 14th, when hearing the small-pox was very rife in and about London, and Lady Browne having a desire to drink Tunbridge waters, I carried them thither, and staied in a very sweete place, private and refreshing, and tooke the waters myself till the 23rd, when I went to prepare for their reception, leaving them for ye present in their little cottage by the Wells.'

The Evelyns returned again in July. In August 1661, when he was back again visiting his wife, who was there for her health, he

> '. . . greately admired the extravagant turnings, insinuations, and growth of certaine birch trees among the rocks'.

In July 1663, the seal of fashion was set on the Wells by a visit from Charles II and his Queen. During the Great Plague of London in 1665, many of the nobility made it their headquarters and the King and Queen held Court there in July 1666. Macaulay, in his *History of England*, refers to these visits of the Court and says that 'during the season a kind of fair was held daily near the fountain . . .' and that '. . . milliners, toymen and jewellers came down from London and opened a bazaar under the trees'. Doubtless the local shopkeepers were not content to see the visitors to their fashionable spa buying from itinerant vendors and they soon augmented their permanent shops and developed locally made, speciality woodware, suitable for souvenirs. Among the 'toys' for which Tunbridge Wells was then already famed, were miniature yew wood tea sets made from local wood, the manufacture of which was continued into the present century.

In 1688, Princess Anne, wife of the Prince of Denmark, was at the Wells, which she visited several times during the next ten years. The area now known as The Pantiles was first laid out between 1660 and 1700 and was first called The Walks and then The Promenade. In 1700, it was paved with Dutch 'pan' tiles (tiles baked in shallow pans) and it then became known as The Pantiles. The tiling was commanded and paid for by Princess Anne in 1697; the delay in completing this work lost the inhabitants the favour and patronage of the Princess, who refused to visit the Wells after 1698.

That inveterate 'spaw' visitor and sampler of medicinal water, Celia Fiennes, often visited the fashionable 'Wells'. She was there in 1697 and, after referring to the many good lodgings now erected and the excellent market for food, described the

'. . . shopps full of all sorts of toys, silver, china, milliners, and all sorts of curious wooden ware, which this place is noted for the delicate neate and thin ware of wood both white and Lignum vitæ wood . . .'.

The reference to the dense and handsomely marked, imported lignum vitae, which was supposed to impart curative medicinal qualities to the contents of wassail bowls and dipper cups, then in vogue, also mortars, makes one wonder if these delights of the wealthy and fashionable were among the 'toys' to be bought at the Wells.

Royalty continued to visit the spa in the eighteenth century. In 1739

[23]

Frederick Prince of Wales and his Princess were there and in 1765 the Dukes of York and Gloucester were visitors.

In 1762, Samuel Derrick, critic, editor of *Dryden* and friend of Dr. Johnson, wrote words which unfortunately are still true of many of our fashions:

'Were this [the ware] smuggled abroad and then imported as a foreign commodity, I am persuaded that people would run after it, but alas! everyone knows it is English and the encouragement is therefore poor.'

Derrick also records sending as a present to a friend, a dressing box and set of toilet boxes of Tunbridge ware, inlaid with highly polished yew, cherry, holly and other woods of which 'the neighbourhood yields great plenty'. Derrick could probably have bought his Tunbridge ware in London by this time, for the products had acquired such fame that London turners were stocking it. In his 1766 *History of Tunbridge Wells*, Benge Burr wrote

'The trade of Tunbridge-Wells is similar to that of the Spa in Germany, and chiefly consists in a variety of toys in wood, such as tea-chests, dressing-boxes, snuff-boxes, punch-ladles, and numerous other little articles of the same kind. Of these great quantities are sold to the company in the summer, and especially at their leaving the place, when it is customary for them to take Tunbridge fairings to their friends at home.

This ware takes its name from the place, on account of its employing a great number of hands, and being made there in a much neater manner than any where else in England. The wood principally used for this purpose is holly, which grows in great abundance in the surrounding country, and furnishes a prodigious variety of the prettiest ornamental inlays that can be imagined, some of which are so excellent in their kind, that it is hard to believe they are not assisted by the pencil. But, besides holly, they use no small quantity of cherry-tree, plum-tree, yew, and sycamore: the yew especially is of late become very fashionable, and the goods vineered with it are certainly excessively pretty.'

In 1799, Fanny Burney was attracted by the Tunbridge ware on sale at the shops in The Pantiles.

[24]

Sir Ambrose Heal's invaluable *London Furniture Makers 1660–1840* shows the trade cards of John Alexander, Ivory and Hard Wood Turner, who practised his calling at the 'Elephant and Coffee Mill' in Crooked Lane between 1776 and 1793 and who sold 'Tunbridge Toys', and Gerard Crawly, Turner, who was at the 'Coffee Mill and Nimble Ninepence' in Cornhill in 1768 and there sold 'Tunbridge and all other Turnery Wares'. Sir Ambrose also includes the trade card of Thomas Jaques, of 65 Leather Lane, 'Manufacturer of Ivory, Hard-woods, Bone and Tunbridge Ware—Wholesale & for Exportation', and gives the date *circa* 1790. In our London directories, we have traced that in 1821 the title of the firm changed to T. & J. Jaques and Tunbridge ware continued to be mentioned as one of their lines until 1835, when reference to the ware had dropped out and been replaced by desk, dressing case and work-box manufacturers.

Two other dealers in Tunbridge ware in the pre-mosaic period, of whom we have record, are I. or J. Robinson and Malcolm Dunnett, both of whom were in business over several years. Robinson was at 53 Piccadilly from 1802, but by 1810 had moved to 51 Piccadilly and in 1812 to Margaret Street, Cavendish Square, where he remained until at least 1817; he also had premises at Tunbridge Wells, about which further details are given in the next chapter. Malcolm Dunnett was at 154 Cheapside in 1802, described as a perfumer and toyman. From 1805, he was at 3 Cheapside, and in 1808 the first reference to the business as Tunbridge and toy warehouse occurs and continues until 1825. In 1812, Dunnett's Toy and Tunbridge Ware Repository advertised their new season's stock, also stating 'Tunbridge Ware repaired and varnished'. By 1832, the description against Malcolm Dunnett had changed to importer of Dutch toys.

We have been unable to establish whether any of the above London traders were actually manufacturers of the ware or only stocked it as one of their lines, but it seems more likely that Dunnett, at any rate, was only a stockist.

Eighteenth-century Tunbridge ware was quite expensive: Sir John Filmer of East Sutton Park, Maidstone, records, in April 1766, 'Paid for a Tunbridge Ware Work Box for M. Filmer (his niece, Mary Filmer) £1.4.0.' That sum would have to be multiplied probably fifteen times to represent the equivalent price today.

There is no doubt that Tunbridge ware was sufficiently good and distinctive to enjoy, like the spa itself, considerable local fame in the early seventeenth century and a national reputation in the late seventeenth and eighteenth centuries. We also know that, in the main, it was small cabinet work and turnery and that some of it was inlaid, but no seventeenth- or eighteenth-century makers, so far as we know, put their names on their ware. Other snippets of information which have survived show that some Tunbridge woodware was decorated with paint. In fact, the picture which is built up is of a highly skilled, well-organized, local woodworking industry, consisting of turners, cabinet makers, veneer hands, marquetry workers and painters in oils, specializing in small decorative woodware, in a wide price range, for souvenirs for visitors to the Wells, and changing their technique according to the prevailing fashion.

Thus, for their best work, they may have commenced with floral marquetry in Charles II's reign and then changed over to arabesque marquetry and oyster shell veneering. In the early eighteenth century, they probably used lacquer and later records show that they treated wood in imitation of tortoiseshell. In the last quarter of the eighteenth century, they are known to have executed inlaid work in the Sheraton style. Probably during all these periods, they made their cheaper articles of white woods, varnish coated and decorated with coloured paint lines and simple designs—geometric, floral or Oriental, according to fashion, taste and the purse. That they also supplied 'in the white' woodware for their customers to decorate is proved by the following advertisement in the *Maidstone Journal*, February 27, 1810—

'WANTED a Man and a Boy in the Tunbridge-Ware Line——— The Man will be required to make White Wood Boxes in the best manner for Ladies to paint on; the Boy to make Sliding, Puzzle Boxes and other small Articles: and both may have constant employment.'

Plate 5 shows examples of the kinds of high grade veneered and inlaid woodware which were made at Tunbridge Wells between 1775 and 1820, when sharply contrasting veneers were in fashion. Although there is no documentary proof that any of these pieces were actually sold as Tunbridge ware, the fact that some parts of the inlaid designs used in nearly all of them are found again in later pieces which also contain Tunbridge wood mosaic, may be considered fairly conclusive.

Inlaid cribbage and other games boards, like the four in the top row, were early specialities of Tonbridge and Tunbridge Wells. Cube pattern inlay is seen on the card case and the paper weight in the bottom row and on a box in the middle row, where it combines with vandyke pattern. Both these *inlay* designs continued in favour as centres to the later end grain *mosaic* until the end of the nineteenth century, and cube pattern was revived in this century. The spill vases, turned from solid rings of various coloured woods, are unusual and probably *circa* 1800. The salt box between them is late eighteenth century.

Plate 7 shows the less expensive, paint decorated woodware, of the type sold as 'Tunbridge' between 1790 and 1820 or 1830. All are made of natural woods, clear polished or varnished and decorated with oil paint—black, green and red usually being the preponderating decorative colours. The Regency cottage ornée is amusingly portrayed in the sewing clamp labelled 'A present from Tunbridge Wells', which is screwed on the adjustable candle stand, top left of the picture, and in the combined candle holder and tinder box on the right. Many Regency trifles made at Tunbridge Wells bear a label saying 'A present from . . .', the places including Tunbridge Wells, or Brighton, or Margate, etc., but some substitute the word 'trifle' for 'present'. The two cup and ball sticks, a late variant of *bilboquet*, echo the green palm leaf decoration of the columns in the kitchens of the Brighton Pavilion.

Cribbage and Pope Joan boards and games markers were also available in this inexpensive ware; examples are shown in Plate 7. The view on the cribbage board is of the chain pier, Brighton. Brighton, during the Regency, was probably a larger market for Tunbridge ware than Tunbridge Wells itself. The circular wooden spice box, bottom right, is the ancestor of the japanned iron one, beloved of Victorians. The toilet boxes in the top row, one surmounted by a ring holder, date from 1790. The other objects in the picture are Regency period.

There were a number of south coast resort stockists of the woodware, amongst whom were those listed in Appendix I; some of their labels may be found on Tunbridge ware and later ones on mosaic, but it is probable that few of them were genuine manufacturers. As will be seen in the next chapter, however, two of them operating in the mosaic period, Medhurst of Weymouth and Green of Rye, were both definitely makers.

CHAPTER TWO

The Range of Objects & the Makers of Tunbridge Ware & Tunbridge Mosaic

AS STATED in the previous chapter, the Tunbridge woodworking industry already had several centuries of tradition in woodware behind it before the introduction of the wood mosaic. In consequence, the range of woodwork became considerably larger than that of the Scottish souvenir ware, which is the subject of Part II of this book. Moreover, many items, such as inkstands, work boxes, games boxes, stamp boxes, pincushions, needle cases, etc., were made in a very wide variety of shapes and designs, affording great scope for collectors. Additionally, the inlaid furniture which had been made at Tunbridge in the eighteenth century, continued to be made as occasional rarities in the nineteenth century, sometimes with the addition of centrepieces or borders of the mosaic. Such furniture—tea-poys, games and work tables, fire screens and, even more rarely, chairs—has sometimes the main part of the decoration in cube, vandyke or other traditional inlays, with the addition of bird or butterfly mosaic centres, or mosaic banded borders. Smaller objects, such as miniature chests of drawers and various fitted caskets and boxes, show similar traditional decoration.

Cube and vandyke inlay designs may date any time from about 1790 onwards, but whereas they were used as the main decoration in the eighteenth century, they became centrepieces of mosaic bordered objects, or borders of objects with mosaic centres, throughout the nineteenth century, and cube pattern was revived again in the 1930s by T. L. Green of Rye. During the nineteenth century, the borders of cube pattern objects gradually became more elaborate and complex. They commenced with plain stringings or simple bandings, then went on to geometric bandings and from there to elaborate 'Berlin woolwork' floral bandings. Late nineteenth-century work is sometimes found with several bandings on an object, including all the above. Green's twentieth-century Rye mosaic went back to the early nineteenth century in its simplicity.

Butterfly and bird mosaic centres, said to have been first devised by the Burrows family, were a *tour de force* on expensive work from the late 1820s until at least the Great Exhibition of 1851. They can only be judged for date by consideration of the whole design, particularly the border or borders. Floral mosaic centres were largely used from about 1845; castles, abbeys, ruins and architectural subjects in general were favoured throughout the second half of the nineteenth century; dog mosaic centres enjoyed a vogue in the 1870s.

Early borders of all subjects consisted of plain, contrasting stringings or bandings, which changed to mosaic bandings in the 1830s and Berlin floral 'woolwork' bandings around 1845. The Berlin patterns retained their popularity during the rest of the nineteenth century and were frequently used in addition to geometric mosaic bandings on the same object.

Stickware, which is described in the next chapter, was used alone and in conjunction with mosaic slices throughout the nineteenth century.

The most popular backgrounds all through the nineteenth century were rosewood, bird's-eye maple, both natural and coloured grey by immersion in the chalybeate water, sycamore similarly treated, walnut and holly.

The following list of Tunbridge ware and Tunbridge mosaic objects comprises those which have been collected or seen by us, but it must be emphasized that there are many varieties of most of them.

Banjos	Book slides	Candlesticks
Bilboquets	Brooches	Card cases
Blotter books	Caddy spoons	Chairs
Bonnet stands	Cake baskets	Cheroot cases
Book markers	Candle arms	Chests, miniature
Book rests	Candle stands	Clothes brushes

Coin collectors' cabinets
Compass cases
Counter boxes
Cribbage boards
Darning eggs
Desk boxes
Ell rules
Emery cushions
Étuis
Games boxes
Games markers
Glove boxes
Hall letter boxes
Handkerchief boxes
Hatpin heads
Inkstands
Jewel boxes and caskets
Kettle holders
Knitting needle protectors
Knitting sheaths
Match boxes
Match stands
Medicine chests
Miniature furniture
Money boxes
Mosaic pictures
Needle books
Needle cases

Needlework clamps
Newspaper rests
Notebook cases
Organs
Paper knives
Pen and pencil cylindric boxes
Pen holders
Pen stands
Pen trays
Pen wipers
Pencils
Photograph albums
Photograph and picture frames
Pincushions
Pin poppets
Playing card boxes
Pope Joan boards
Postcard boxes
Puzzle boxes
Reel boxes
Reticule frames
Ring stands
Rouge pots
Rulers
Screens
Sealing wax outfits
Serviette rings
Sewing compendiums
Shawl pins

Silk ball holders
Silk-skein holders
Silk winders
Smelling salts bottle cases
Sovereign boxes
Spectacle cases
Spice boxes
Spill vases
Spinning tops
Stamp boxes
Stationery cabinets
String holders
Tape measure cases
Taper cases
Taper holders
Tea caddies
Tea-poys
Thermometer stands
Thimble cases
Thread waxers
Tobacco barrels
Toilet boxes
Trays
Trick opening boxes
Trinket stands
Watch stands
Work boxes
Writing boxes
Writing desks
Yo-yos

Certain tidy-minded people have named the exact date of invention and the name of the inventor of Tunbridge wood mosaic; they have also assessed the rival claims of makers in Tonbridge and Tunbridge Wells to the invention. Unfortunately, they do not agree on any of these points. We have only been investigating for twenty-four years and we have come to the conclusion that we commenced our research over a century too late to be absolutely sure that we have elicited the truth, the whole truth and nothing but the truth.

One of the writers who was particularly confusing on dates was Henry R. Knife, whose *Tunbridge Wells and Neighbourhood* was published in 1916. He said

> 'At the end of the 18th century, the manufacture of Tunbridge Ware was commenced in Tunbridge Wells itself in an old tower situate in the grounds of what is now the Spa Hotel. Soon after this, the firm of Fenner and Nye was formed and commenced manufacture at what was then, and until a few years ago, known as the Repository on Mount Ephraim. This building is now better known as the Chalet, and the sale of goods made there was carried on in an old building which stood close to the present gateway of Mount Ephraim House. On the death of Fenner the property became the subject of a Chancery suit and was subsequently purchased by the late Mr. Elers who resided at Mount Ephraim House for many years.'

This is considerably more than one hundred years too late for the origin of Tunbridge ware and perhaps twenty-five or thirty years too early for the mosaic. Nevertheless, we assume it does refer to the mosaic and we think that Knife may have been correct about the work having commenced in the old tower in the grounds of what is now the Spa Hotel. One day, when we were researching at Tunbridge Wells, a young collector, Francis Taylor, brought us for identification a cribbage board decorated with a Tunbridge mosaic picture of an old building and a ruined tower. Pictorially, the subject is dull compared with the usual architectural subjects, so it may well have been made because of the local historical interest.

There are or were in the district several families whose names appear as leading manufacturers of the ware and later of the mosaic, generation after generation. Many of these families, in a small community, were inevitably related by marriage. They also formed and dissolved partnerships and one may find names of competitors who came together as partners for a time, and then for a second time traded as separate businesses under their individual names. All this complicates research.

When we commenced our work, we were able to interview some surviving members of the old mosaic and woodware families. We were most fortunate, too, in that the late Dr. Given, the then honorary curator of Tunbridge Wells Museum, who had been interviewing other leading families for many years, allowed us to study his notes. Perhaps this is also the place to insert our appreciation of the co-operation of the late Mrs. E. Bradley, Dr. Given's successor, and our indebtedness to Mr. R. G. Sandbach, MA, the present curator, who has given us every facility for research and has generously added to our knowledge by his findings. Finally, we were able to interview and check some of our technical findings with Mr. Albert Frank Hemsley who, as a boy, was apprenticed in 1917 to Boyce, Brown & Kemp, one of the last surviving makers of the mosaic.

From our own and Dr. Given's research we learned a lot about the trade customs and technicalities in the various workshops, but nothing about the origin of the mosaic; this was because nearly every person interviewed stated that his or her ancestor was the inventor, and this tradition was unshakable. Before discussing the various local claimants to the invention of the mosaic and the conclusion which we eventually reached, we must have a European digression.

The continental 'Spa', which gave its name to the mineral bath centres elsewhere, was known for its chalybeate and alkaline springs as early as the fourteenth century and became famous as a health resort at the beginning of the seventeenth century. Like Tunbridge Wells, the town quickly developed a range of wooden souvenir knick-knacks, but instead of platters and other turnery, it commenced with walking sticks and canes, quite a necessity for visitors traversing the very steep paths leading to the various springs. From this modest beginning, there developed in Spa a range very similar to Tunbridge ware in the eighteenth century and among its finishes were included painted, inlaid, lacquered and pen-and-ink decorated ware. The pen-and-ink decorated ware influenced Scottish ware, as will be seen in Part II of this book, and it is quite likely that the other finishes influenced Tunbridge manufacturers. Because of this, it has been said that the ingenious method of making Tunbridge wood mosaic came from Spa. Nothing is more unlikely, because not only is the mosaic unlike Spa work in style and general taste but, moreover, there never seems to have been any wood mosaic in the Spa range, although the local woodware goes on being made and sold to this day.

If a foreign introduction is sought as the source of Tunbridge wood mosaic, then the Mediterranean basin is the area in which antiquity of the craft and of geometric patterns will be found. Persian Shiraz, Damascus, Egyptian, Moorish and early Italian mosaic all bear some visual resemblance to Tunbridge, but only the first, so far as we know, employed the ingenious Tunbridge method which obviated the necessity of having to lay all the tesserae separately. Nevertheless, nineteenth-century Italians in the neighbourhood of Sorrento and Amalfi did develop precisely the same method as Tunbridge and they are still successfully making Sorrento wood mosaic souvenirs in their family workshops.

Sorrento wood mosaic was inaugurated by Antonia Damora and Luigi Garguilo in 1827. Tunbridge wood mosaic must have commenced about the same time. Because there are some Italian names on tombstones in local Tunbridge churchyards, it has been deduced that Italian workers introduced the mosaic method to Tunbridge. It is a poor deduction; the tombstones prove nothing more than that there were Italians, or people of Italian descent, living in the vicinity. The mysterious Italian wood mosaic worker or workers have never been identified. Recently, a barometer in Tunbridge wood mosaic frame came to light in an American collection. It bore the name P. Rosapini, and at first sight it looked as if it might be the missing link between Sorrento and Tunbridge mosaic. However, the fact that the name was on the barometer dial, and not on the back of the Tunbridge case, made us suspicious and we soon tracked down P. Rosapini as a jeweller in Frant Road, Tunbridge Wells. Doubtless he bought in the fashionable wood mosaic cases for the barometers, which he sold under his own name.

There is no way of being sure whether Tunbridge wood mosaic antedated the similarly made Sorrento mosaic or whether it followed it by a few years. There is also the distinct possibility that coincidentally the same idea was worked up simultaneously by two people far apart, who knew nothing of each other's work, as occurred with aluminium, and with electric lamps. Judged on design, the earliest Tunbridge wood mosaic could be a few years earlier than 1827, but it cannot be proved.

Some Sorrento mosaic can easily be confused, and often is, with Tunbridge mosaic. The early Sorrento work is just as fine as anything made at Tunbridge, but the geometric lines are often wavy and there is greater use made of woods dyed in various colours. To assist identification, we include in colour Plate 2, some examples of nineteenth-century Sorrento work.

We now give some details of the principal makers of Tunbridge mosaic, with notes of those who are claimed to have been the inventor, and our conclusions on this question.

Tonbridge Makers

Wise   George Wise of Tonbridge is believed to have been established as a turner in 1685 and the Wise family were the leading family of wholesale and retail woodware manufacturers in Tonbridge until the death of 62-year-old John Wise, the last survivor of the family business, in 1899. The Wise showroom, with workshops behind it, was in Tonbridge High Street, on the corner of the bridge over the Medway. An old print picturing it, is reproduced in Fig. 1. Wise's small ware, labelled 'A Present from . . .' is believed

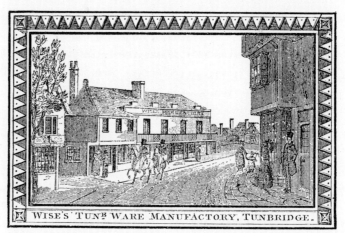

WISE'S TUN^B WARE MANUFACTORY, TUNBRIDGE.

Fig. 1. Wise's premises beside the river bridge in Tonbridge High Street. Early nineteenth century.

to have been widely sold in seaside resorts and inland spas in the United Kingdom over a long period. During the nineteenth century, Wise had other showrooms at 11 Calverley Parade and at The Parade, Tunbridge Wells. John Wise's wife, Frances, born in 1841, was the daughter of Robert Russell, one of the leading manufacturers of marquetry and mosaic in Tunbridge Wells. Most of this information was obtained in 1951 from 85-year-old Agnes Anne Wise, daughter of John and Frances. Miss Wise named Robert Russell

[34]

as the inventor of the marquetry (mosaic?) and as the maker of the reading stand presented to Princess Victoria in 1826—for other accounts of this reading stand, see *Fenner*, also *Russell*.

Presumably confusing the oldest maker of Tonbridge *ware* with the oldest makers of Tonbridge or Tunbridge *mosaic*, some writers have named the Wise family as inventors of the mosaic, but this claim does not seem to have been made at any time by the Wise family; they were, however, certainly making woodware on a large scale in Tonbridge throughout the eighteenth century. Before they made wood mosaic, they, like most of the other makers, specialized in such objects as tea caddies, work boxes, cribbage and Pope Joan boards, etc., veneered with satin or holly wood and inlaid, or painted with narrow coloured lines; examples of this ware are shown in Plates 5 and 7. Later examples had floral or shell details painted in or sometimes inlaid against backgrounds of contrasting veneers.

One of the several members of the Wise family with the Christian name of George, who is believed to have lived *circa* 1780–1864, seems to have been a talented designer. Some 23 accomplished water colour designs for marquetry work, painted by him and dated 1806 to 1814, have recently come to light and have been purchased by Tunbridge Wells Museum.

Other Tonbridge Makers   Other Tonbridge makers recorded are John Nye and Zachariah Cox, who were advertising between 1823 and 1840; we have traced no other details about them.

Tunbridge Wells Makers

Jordan   Contemporary with George Wise of Tonbridge, a man named Jordan is said to have commenced the manufacture of Tunbridge ware at Jordan's Place, Tunbridge Wells, in 1685. The name Jordan as a manufacturer occurs again in records of 1720, but nothing is known of either Jordan.

Fenner and *Nye*   Fenner and Nye are two of the most prominent names in Tunbridge ware and high class Tunbridge wood mosaic and they manufactured on a large scale at Tunbridge Wells. They commenced business separately and then came together as the partnership, Fenner & Nye. This partnership must have continued through two or three generations; when the partners separated, each traded again under his own name. Edmund Nye, of Fenner & Nye, was presumably related to Sarah Nye, Tunbridge ware dealer, and John Nye of Tonbridge, manufacturer, both trading around 1823.

Fenner was established at the Chalet, Mount Ephraim, in 1720 and the partnership, Fenner & Nye, occupied the same premises; the partnership is believed to have been dissolved about 1825. Fenner & Co. were still advertising, and showing the Royal Warrant, at the Chalet, Mount Ephraim, up to 1840 and Fenner specifically advertised mosaic and inlaid woodwork. In May, 1837, the following advertisement appeared—

'MOSAIC AND INLAID WOOD FURNITURE. . . . Fenner & Co. of Mount Ephraim (Manufacturers to their Majesties & the Royal Family) beg to acquaint the Nobility, Gentry & others that they have taken rooms, 209 Regent Street (London) for the purpose of exhibiting for sale their extensive and novel manufacture . . .'

Although the combined reading, writing stand and work box presented to Princess Victoria by the inhabitants of Tunbridge Wells on the occasion of her seventh birthday in 1826, has been attributed to Russell, it was, according to John Colbran, writing only thirteen years later, by Fenner. The following is Colbran's interesting account—

'. . . in the year 1826, the inhabitants wishing to present the Princess Victoria with an article of their staple commodity, entered into a subscription for the purpose. This subscription was limited to five shillings each person, which shortly amounted to twenty-five guineas, raised exclusively by the inhabitants. As it was thought that a feeling of jealousy might be created by selecting one manufacturer, it was agreed that Mr. William Fenner, Mr. Edmund Nye, Messrs. Sharp, and Mr. James Friend should draw lots for the appointment. This was accordingly done, and Mr. Fenner was the successful candidate. Under the direction of the committee he prepared the following handsome present: A table formed with King-wood, beautifully veneered with party-coloured woods from every part of the globe. It was lined with gold tufted satin, and comprised a complete writing and reading desk, covered with purple embossed velvet, fitted up with cut glasses mounted in massive silver. A side drawer exhibited a complete work-box, with appropriate instruments of richly-chased silver; the reels, runners, &c. being of sandal wood, and the silk winders fine specimens of native and foreign woods; the whole lined throughout with gold-coloured embossed satin. A drawer on the opposite side was furnished with a drawing box, comprising the necessary colours, pencils, pallet, sandal-wood rulers, &c. From the lower part of the top a work-box of rich gold-coloured silk, appropriately ornamented, fell in graceful folds. The whole was supported by a finely-worked tripod of solid King-wood: and altogether it was considered an unique specimen of the taste and ingenuity of Tunbridge-ware manufacturers.'

The Princess, with her mother the Duchess of Kent, spent many of her girlhood holidays—1822, 1826, 1827, 1834, 1835—staying at Mount Pleasant House, now the Calverley Hotel.

MOSAIC & INLAID WOOD WORK.

FENNER & CO.

Manufacturers to Her Majesty, & the Royal Family,

Beg to acquaint the Nobility, Gentry, and the Public, that at their Manufactory, *(the oldest and only extensive one in the trade,)* they have always on hand a very large assortment of Mosaic and Inlaid Wood Work, consisting of Tables for various uses, Tea Poys, Work, Drawing, and Card Boxes. Flower Vases, Tea Caddies, and numerous other articles peculiar to their Establishment, which they are Selling at very reduced prices, owing to the introduction of new Machinery.

Mount Ephraim, Tunbridge Wells.

Fig. 2. Fenner & Co.'s advertisement, 1839–40.

Fenner & Co.'s advertisement in the 32-page advertisement section at the end of Colbran's *Guide* is worth giving in detail and is reproduced in Fig. 2.

Edmund Nye, trading as 'Late Fenner & Nye', advertised in 1840, with premises at the Parade and manufactory in adjoining Market Place. His advertisement stated: 'An elegant assortment constantly on Sale—Goods repaired and re-varnished.' This statement disposes of the fiction that all early mosaic was polished and the later work varnished. Nye was in business at least until 1851. After his death or retirement, the business was carried on by Thomas Barton.

'An endless variety of Inlaid and Mosaic Tunbridge-Ware' was amongst the items named in an 1840 advertisement of 'Nye's Select Theological Circulating Library; Wholesale and Retail Stationery, Book, Tunbridge-Ware and Toy Warehouse' at 7 & 8 Grosvenor Road, Tunbridge Wells, but we consider that this Nye was a stockist, not a manufacturer.

Barton   Thomas Barton, successor to Edmund Nye, was born in 1819 and died in 1902. Presumably he was descended from or related to John Barton, who is said to have been making inlaid Tunbridge ware at Mount Ephraim in 1728. Thomas Barton was an apprentice of Wise of Tonbridge and joined Nye about 1836. Barton is reputed to have designed Nye's chromatrope table, which contained 129,540 wood tesserae and won a medal at the 1851 Exhibition. Barton was a fine designer and technician and raised the quality of Tunbridge mosaic of the late period to its highest level. He became an alderman and a partner of Nye, trading for a time as Barton & Nye, and after Nye's death in 1863, and until 1902, he carried on successfully as 'Thomas Barton, late Nye', or sometimes with the label 'Thomas Barton'. Like most of the other makers, Barton sometimes used gummed paper labels on his ware, but in some instances he used a rubber stamp.

In 1931, on the demolition of an old building in Tunbridge Wells, a collection of boxes containing old Tunbridge patterns, blocks, gauges and documents came to light. On investigation, the hoard proved to be the original patterns, assembled and partially assembled blocks and specimens of rare woods and fine coloured veneers of the noted eighteenth-century ware and nineteenth-century wood mosaic manufacturers, Fenner & Nye, who turned out some of the finest pieces. The collection had been lying forgotten and undisturbed since the closing down of the business on Alderman Barton's death or retirement. The accumulation, which was sold by auction by Brackett & Sons of Tunbridge Wells on February 24, 1933, included the original late eighteenth-century jig-saw, and the turning tools used in making both Tunbridge ware and mosaic. The jig-saw, treadle operated and mostly made of mahogany, said to have been made by W. Fenner about 1760, is shown in Plate 8. The cylinder on the top contains a powerful spring. The machine, which is still in working order, was used for fretting out the eighteenth-century marquetry designs. Unfortunately, some patterns and historical documents were sold to America, but we purchased the above-mentioned jig-saw, some tools and gauges, many specimens of woods used in the mosaic and a selection of blocks, patterns and templates, and some of the assembly charts and coloured designs illustrated here.

Burrows   The Burrows brothers, William, James, George and Humphrey, were amongst the most important of the Tunbridge manufacturers. Their grandfather, William or James Burrows, is said to have commenced making the ware at Gibraltar Cottage, Tunbridge Wells, some accounts say in 1685, others in 1720. George and James in partnership were at The Parade, Culverden Cottage, Ephraim Terrace, and Hanover Lodge, between 1820 and about 1842; James also had his grandfather's premises at Gibraltar Cottage, The Common, in 1820. William was in the High Street between 1820 and 1847 and was recorded at Southborough in 1870, but this last recording may refer to a son or nephew. A print, dated 1822, shows Her Royal Highness, later Queen Victoria, returning from a morning ride on a donkey, at Tunbridge Wells; in the background is Jordan House, the double-fronted shop of Humphrey Burrows. The shop is sign-written 'Original Manufactory of Tunbridge Ware, Burrows'.

James and George Burrows, who traded wholesale and retail, claimed to be the inventors or originators of the mosaic and we think their claim is substantiated by the following evidence. In 1840, John Colbran published *A New Guide for Tunbridge Wells*, from which we have already quoted. This guide was written in 1839, or perhaps earlier—anyway, we deduce, within a dozen or so years of the introduction of the mosaic. Colbran has a chapter headed *Manufacture* and, after referring to the similarity of the early ware to that of Spa, and the making of humming tops and small turnery, he goes on to say—

'Encouraged by their extraordinary success, the art obtained a wider range, and instead of the simple wood, other and more adventurous spirits attempted greater things. This led to the introduction of veneering,

[39]

and afterwards, from an accidental occurrence, the present mosaic system was acted upon. It was introduced in the following manner. Mr. James Burrows, whose grandfather had been one of the chief manufacturers, or perhaps the only one in the neighbourhood, was attracted by a row of wooden beads, worn by a lady, which did not correspond with the colours of her dress; thinking that something of the kind might be effected in Tunbridge-ware, of different woods combined, he eventually produced a necklace of the mosaic work, for which he received two guineas from a lady then residing at Cumberland Terrace, accompanied with an order for another. This acting as a stimulus upon his inventive faculties, he turned his attention more particularly to the improvement of the ware, and has succeeded, we believe, beyond his most sanguine expectations. Mr. Burrows was the first to introduce butterflies and birds into this description of manufacture. Such is the value set upon Tunbridge-ware articles, that few persons visit the place without purchasing for their friends some reminiscence of it, which is considered acceptable . . .'

Moreover, at the end of the *Guide* there are 32 pages of advertisements which include the following Tunbridge ware and mosaic manufacturers: Edmund Nye (late Fenner & Nye); Fenner & Co. (by Royal Appointment); H. Burrows; I. J. & A. Sharp (by Royal Appointment); G. & J. Burrows. G. & J. Burrows' advertisement is reproduced in Fig. 3 and it will be noted that they claim to be '*Inventors of the Mosaic Inlaid Ware*'. This is as near as we have been able to get to contemporary evidence and as none of Burrows' competitors seem to have contested their claim at the time, we think it is pretty conclusive that they were the first and that all other claims originated later. As a matter of interest, in 1949 we met old William Burrows, whose family had handed down the tradition that his great-grandfather was the inventor. The family also claimed that one of their apprentices taught mosaic manufacture to Wise of Tonbridge. When William Burrows died in 1952, we bought some of his collection of the mosaic.

H. Burrows Jun.'s advertisement gives his address as 'Royal Tunbridge Ware Repository and Manufactory, Jordan Place, London Road' and states 'Established 1685'. The first Burrows of Jordan Place may have become the shadowy Jordan of Jordan Place, as the dates are the same. If this be so, it

G. & J. BURROWS,

(Inventors of the Mosaic Inlaid Ware,)

PARADE, TUNBRIDGE WELLS,

AND

CULVERDEN COTTAGE, EPHRAIM TERRACE.

Manufacturers of Tunbridge Ware, Wholesale and Retail.

A great assortment of Inlaid Turnery, of the Newest Inventions.

MANUFACTORY, HANOVER ROAD.

Fig. 3. G. & J. Burrows' advertisement, 1839–40, claiming the invention of the mosaic.

looks as though the Burrows family were probably the first in Tunbridge Wells with both the ware and the mosaic.

Russell Another first class maker was Robert Russell, of Vale Place, Tunbridge Wells, who mixed mosaic with a distinctive and possibly unique marquetry of his own designing. Examples of some of his unusual and attractive boxes are shown in Plate 25. As will be noted, the patterns are quite different from those of his competitors. Russell specialized in decorating his work with marquetry of tulip wood and also local woods, such as holly, furze, laburnum, and other strikingly marked timbers, brought to him by arrangement with local gardeners. Robert Russell was born in 1812; his

[41]

father had a Tunbridge ware shop in the London Road. In his young days, Robert was apprenticed to Fenner & Nye. He then opened up on his own and later had two sons and some apprentices in his prosperous business. He exhibited at the 1851 Exhibition and was awarded a bronze medal for a lady's work box. The Royal Arms appear in his later advertisements. He was an advertiser in Brackett's 1863 *Shilling Guide to Tunbridge Wells* and in 1864 he exhibited in a local exhibition at Tunbridge Wells.

As mentioned under *Wise*, Robert Russell's daughter married John Wise, and apparently their granddaughter also married into the Wise family, for she, Mrs. Maude E. Wise, writing in 1927 to a Mr. Howard (by permission of whose nephew Mr. M. Howard, we quote), said that Robert Russell

'. . . invented Tunbridge Ware Marquetry which gained the highest award in the Exhibition of 1851. This brought him more orders from America than he could possibly execute, it being all his own and two sons' handwork. He had apprentices, of course, but they could not do the artistic work. He served the Royal Family and was allowed to use the Royal Arms. On one occasion he made a beautiful inlaid reading stand for the Duchess of Kent to give her daughter, Queen Victoria, as a birthday gift. He served the Duchess of Kent with many things when she stayed at Eden House on Mount Sion. My Mother has often told us how her Mother and Father would have to go to "Fairlawn", now the Eye and Ear Hospital next to Eden House. Members of the Duchess's household lived there and my grandparents would set out the Tunbridge Ware in a large room there and leave it. Then the Duchess would walk through and select what she wanted and all the business would be done by her Equerry . . .'.

If there is any truth in this story of the presentation reading stand for Princess Victoria, it is obviously not the same stand that was presented in 1826, because Robert Russell was then only aged 14.

Robinson   J. or I. Robinson, active around 1794 until at least 1817, is a name which is rather difficult to fit into the picture and, so far as we know, nothing bearing his label has ever come to light. He described himself as Tunbridge Ware Manufacturer, Print-Seller and Perfumer to Their Royal

Highnesses The Prince and Princess of Wales and The Duke and Duchess of York. Robinson had premises on The Parade, Tunbridge Wells and, as detailed in the previous chapter, he also traded in London. On his broadsheet, he lists the following goods in the order given:

'Perfumes (7 varieties); Essences (14 varieties); Waters (27 varieties); Hair Powders (24 varieties); French Pomatums (25 varieties); Wash Balls (15 varieties); Soaps (13 varieties); For the Teeth—Dentrifices, &c. (13 items); Cosmetics, &c.—and the &c. includes such items as William's new invented Cloth Powder, Shaving Brushes of all sorts, Clothes ditto, Inlaid or Plain, Kennedy and Dr. Lord's Corn Plaister, Steel Hat and Cap Pins, Reeve and Newman's superfine Colors for Drawing, Nail-brushes of all sorts, Court Sticking Plaister, Bailey's Blacking-cakes, Best Cricket-bats and Balls, Shoe-traps, &c., Broomhead's Razors and Straps, Palmer's ditto, warranted, Reeve, Little, and Scott's True blue, Liquid for cleaning the Tops of Boots and Saddles (36 items in all).'

Then follow the headings Tunbridge Ware, Prints and Medallions, Cork Soles, and winds up with

'A genteel Assortment of Fashionable Trinkets, Silk and Leather Purses, Pocket-Books, Thread-Cases, Smelling-Bottles, Scissors, Penknives, Canes, &c., &c.'

This broadsheet is undated, but must antedate 1810 because on it Robinson's London address is given as 53 Piccadilly and, as we have mentioned in the previous chapter, he was at 51 Piccadilly by 1810.

Whether Robinson actually manufactured the Tunbridge ware which he sold, we do not know, but the list, given below, is interesting as showing the kind of range which was available at the beginning of the nineteenth century.

'Stands for Flowers, with Prints.
York and other Spinning-wheels.
Tables elegantly inlaid with prints.
Dressing and Hand Glasses with ditto.

Writing desks of all sizes with ditto.
Ditto Boxes with ditto.
Work Baskets with ditto.
Ditto Boxes of all sizes, with ditto.
Portable and other Book Shelves.
Dressing and Shaving-Boxes.
Sallad Spoons and Forks.
Card-boxes with counters.
Cribbage-boards and Trays, with ditto.
Boxes of various sizes, fitted complete with
    Reeve, and Newman's colors.
Tea-caddies and Boxes, with Prints or Plain.
Medicine or Cordial-chests, ditto.
Draughts or Backgammon-boards, &c., &c.'

Other Tunbridge Wells Manufacturers   Other makers whose names have been noted and the dates when they appear in directories, are as follows—

W. Foley, Mount Ephraim	1810
George Bennett, Clarence Parade	1839
James & John Cottington, Jordan Place and The Parade	1847
James Friend, The Parade	1823 & 1847
John, James & Ann Sharp, Oldenburgh House, London Road	1823 & 1847
John Stapely, Mount Sion	1847
Alfred Talbot, Chapel Place	1847
Berry Dyer, The Parade	1847
Friend & Allen, 20 & 22 The Parade	1870
Henry Hollamby, 12 The Pantiles, 37 Frant Road and The Parade	1870–1890
Boyce, Brown & Kemp, 108 Camden Road (now renumbered 128–30)	1870 until as late as 1927

William Gasson, of 4 Mountview Villas, Holden Park Road, Southborough (now a suburb of Tunbridge Wells), was active between 1867 and 1891.

Colbran, in his 1840 *Guide*, names Mr. James Friend, Messrs. Sharp, Mr. E. Nye, Messrs. G. & J. Burrows, Mr. H. Burrows, Jun., Messrs. Fenner, and Mr. George Bennett as the principal manufacturers and adds '. . . all of whom feel much pleasure in explaining their mode of manufacture to those visitors who may honor them with a call'.

Henry Hollamby must have been in business in quite a large way, judging by examples of mosaic bearing his label which are still extant. Henry was probably related to John Hollamby of Holden Park Road, Southborough, who was also working around 1891. Both may have been descendants of John Hollamby, carpenter, working at Tonbridge in 1823. Boyce, Brown & Kemp must also have been very active. In their last seven or more years, they traded as Tunbridge Wells Manufacturing Co. and are said to have been controlled from London by David H. E. King (London) Ltd., Table Tennis Manufacturers, of 46 Ufford Street, E.1.

South Coast Resort Manufacturers

At the end of the list of south coast resort stockists, Appendix I, we state that Medhurst of Weymouth and Green of Rye were definitely makers of the mosaic; we now give the basis for this statement.

James Medhurst had come from Tunbridge Wells, and manufactured at Weymouth from *circa* 1846 until some time before 1875. He labelled his mosaic 'A present from Weymouth' and he specialized in using wood from wrecks, giving rather melodramatic accounts of the disasters on boxes, etc., made from the wreckage. Among the wrecked ships from which he made wooden souvenirs were the *Royal George, Columbine* and *Abergavenny*. A floral pattern glove box, $9\frac{1}{2}$ in. by $3\frac{1}{2}$ in., in Tunbridge Wells Museum, is indistinguishable from any of the locally made mosaic, except for Medhurst's label stating that it is made from the wood of the Indiaman, *Abergavenny*, wrecked off Weymouth Bay in February 1805.

Thomas Lyttleton Green, the last maker of the traditional block mosaic, was born at Maidstone in 1892. He served in both World Wars and set up his manufactory at Rye in the inter-war period 1931–9. His 'Mosaic Works' were at Market Road. He made nice, clean, simple geometric designs, with cube pattern very much to the fore. His boxes, such as those for 'MATCHES', 'PINS', 'NEEDLES', etc., had their names lettered in the mosaic on the lids. Green is believed to have been taught the mosaic manufacture by a Mr. Kemp of Tunbridge Wells, probably a member of the Boyce, Brown & Kemp partnership. The Rye works were destroyed by bombing in World War II.

The foregoing information should help collectors in dating their mosaic, but there is one further point worth bearing in mind. Many of the makers had showrooms in The Pantiles. The Pantiles, when first laid out between 1660 and 1700, were known as The Upper and Lower Walks, and then as The Promenade. From 1700 to 1793, they became The Pantiles. From 1793 to 1887, they were known as The Parade. From 1887, they became The Pantiles again. From the point of view of checking dates of labels, it is probably only the nineteenth-century dates which matter.

CHAPTER THREE

The New Mosaic & its Method of Manufacture

WHEN the new method of making mosaic was invented, the Tunbridge ware manufacturers had, for a long while, been producing geometric and mosaic designs of the type shown in Plate 5. But the traditional method of cutting individual pieces of veneer, either singly or in batches of up to 6 in. thickness, to form ornamental sheets of marquetry, was slow, laborious and costly. The new method was much quicker and cheaper and it created the same effects and eventually led to much finer and more intricate designs, such as the selection of original water colour examples shown in Plate 9. The eight narrow strips in the top two lines, and the one at the bottom, dated 1851, were intended for traditional marquetry, or for decorating painted ware; nearly all the others were meant for execution in end grain mosaic.

Once it is realized that the primary objective of the change of technique was *not at first* due to a change of fashion in design, but to a desire to speed up and cheapen production and so increase the market, it becomes clear why the change was accomplished without any flurry of trumpets at the time. People like to buy something at a lower price than they expect, but do not like to learn that it is produced by 'cheap' methods. There was, therefore, no boasting about the new idea until it had become accepted by the customer, and had achieved fame on its own merits through the fineness of the mosaic and the intricate patterns and pictorial effects which it made practical.

[47]

The new method of making the mosaic, probably invented by Burrows during the second decade of the nineteenth century, was, in England at any rate, a revolutionary process for making possible numerous perfect repetitions of a geometric design or picture by a semi-mechanical process.

Briefly, the sticks were selected and assembled in accordance with an assembly chart and a coloured pattern painted on graph paper. In colour Plate 4 are shown a coloured design for a $\frac{3}{4}$-in. wide 'Berlin woolwork' band and the first ten lines of the thirty-eight line chart; the remainder of the design consists of repeats, starting from line 1 again. As he progressed, the operator could check the pattern on the end grain against the painted band, to ensure that he had assembled correctly. Note the date 1843 on the assembly chart. Birmingham Museum possesses an old album of design draw-ings of Nye's and Barton's, some of which are in colour and show 'Berlin woolwork' patterns used between 1851 and 1876.

The assembled block, therefore, consisted of a multiplicity of very fine and accurately cut hardwood sticks of contrasting colours, all of the same length but of varying geometric outlines and sectional dimensions, fitted together in such a manner that running right through the block, from end to end, there was an identical design of mosaic, just as in certain peppermint rock there is lettering. The sticks, after gluing up under pressure, were then sliced transversely into thin veneers of end grain mosaic, which was glued on to the wooden object which it was desired to decorate.

The sequence can be seen in Plate 6. Left, centre, is a bundle of the sticks, all planed to the correct profiles, arranged in the desired pattern, assembled dry, and tightly tied with twine. On the right, is a similar pattern, glued into a block. In front, are a slice off the block, and a finished box lid, with the slice of mosaic glued on. Extreme right is another block, demonstrating the assembly of a banding. Further selections of the end grain mosaic facing patterns, $\frac{1}{16}$ in. thick—the usual thickness—are shown in Plate 10.

Although this ingenious block building and transverse slicing method allowed many repeats from a block, it was not nearly as economical as many people think. Saw-cut veneer is always thicker than knife-cut veneer, and when the mosaic was made there were no knife-cutting machines capable of making the transverse slices of mosaic, so each one had to be cut on a circular saw, and a saw, even a finely ground-off one such as was used, necessarily wastes a lot of wood in sawdust. A recent writer has stated that

5. Although many of these designs may be correctly designated mosaic, they are veneer mosaic, not the nineteenth-century end grain mosaic. *Pinto Collection, Birmingham Museum.*

6. Tunbridge wood mosaic blocks and slices and early examples of mosaic butterfly and bird designs. The blocks, slices and 'bird' casket, *Royal Botanic Gardens, Kew*; the two *circa* 1830 miniature tables, *Pinto Collection, Birmingham Museum*.

7. Examples of the less expensive paint decorated woodware, of the type sold as Tunbridge between 1790 and 1830. *Pinto Collection, Birmingham Museum.*

8. The treadle operated jig-saw, made mostly of mahogany, by W. Fenner, about 1760. *Pinto Collection, Birmingham Museum.*

9. Selection of water-coloured Tunbridge designs. The eight strips in the two top rows and the one dated 1851, at the bottom, were intended for marquetry work. Most of the other designs were for end grain mosaic. *Tunbridge Wells Museum.*

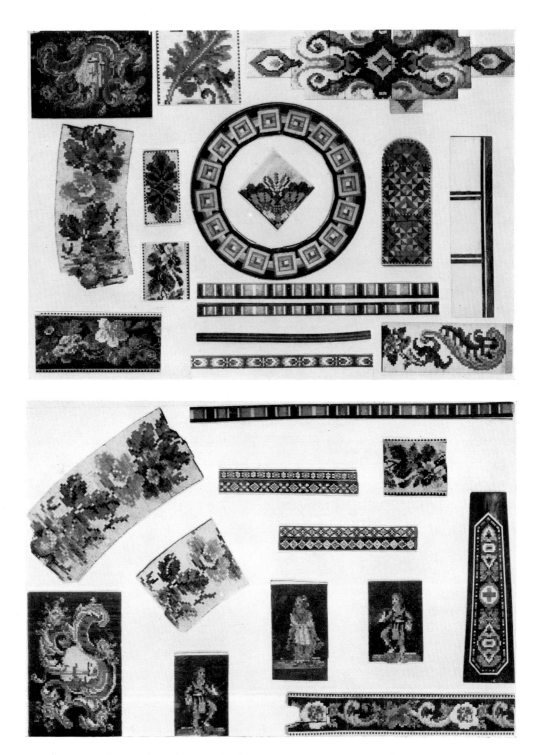

10. Tunbridge end grain mosaic slices from the Fenner and Nye hoard. *Pinto Collection, Birmingham Museum.*

11. Examples of lathe-turned stickware; the watch stands, pen stands and silk-skein holder have end grain mosaic plinths. *Pinto Collection, Birmingham Museum.*

12. Examples of Tunbridge cube pattern—top two rows *circa* 1840, bottom row 1840 to 1890. *Pinto Collection, Birmingham Museum.*

13. Pictorial mosaic, second half of the nineteenth century. Details of the pictures sometimes date them. The Eridge Castle boxes, top left and bottom right, date after 1874; the one top right is earlier. For details—see text. *Pinto Collection, Birmingham Museum.*

14. Fine examples of the end grain mosaic, mostly dating from between 1835 and 1850. The inkstand, on the right, by Edmund Nye, contains nearly 46,000 tesserae and Victoria's head on the stamp box is made up of about 1,000 tesserae; the revolving pencil (standing) has more than 1,600 tesserae. The snuff boxes are all good examples and the sealing wax outfits are much superior to those in Plate 15. *Pinto Collection, Birmingham Museum.*

15. Simple geometric designs made about 1840–5. The yo-yo, top left, and tambour needle case, extreme right, are rather rare. The combined compass and thermometer stand, in the second row, is a good specimen by Barton. The octagonal sealing wax outfits are of poor design. *Pinto Collection, Birmingham Museum.*

16. Boxes, caskets, inkstands and adjustable candle stand, one of a pair, made between 1840 and 1860, when 'Berlin wool' floral mosaic patterns were very popular. The inkstand in front uses the same pattern as the clothes brush in Plate 17. *Pinto Collection, Birmingham Museum.*

17. Further selection of mosaic of the same period as in Plate 16, ranging from fine to coarse. The photograph frame is a poor specimen, made from mosaic 'offcuts'. The rule next to it is well designed and contains some 7,500 tesserae. The miniature table for pins, middle row, is a fine specimen by Barton. The three 'books' in the bottom row are for needles. *Pinto Collection, Birmingham Museum.*

18. A remarkable combination, dial-operated sovereign box, decorated with Tunbridge end grain mosaic. It only opens when the world SURREY is brought into vertical alignment. *Pinto Collection, Birmingham Museum.*

19. Fine Tunbridge mosaic and inlaid marquetry games table, made for Prince Albert by Fenner & Co., about 1845. Now at Kensington Palace. *Reproduced by gracious permission of Her Majesty The Queen.*

20. A remarkable marquetry mosaic table (not end grain), *circa* 1830. *In the Collection of Lord Faringdon, at Buscot Park.*

21. Four out of the seven, all different, mosaic patterned chairs from Lord
Faringdon's Tunbridge marquetry mosaic suite.

22. Selection of fine quality, end grain mosaic, inlaid into bird's-eye maple, stained grey by immersion in chalybeate spring water. The large bookrest, *circa* 1840–45, is an outstanding piece. *Pinto Collection, Birmingham Museum.*

23. An elaborate and fine quality end grain mosaic work table of the mid-nineteenth century, by Edmund Nye. *Tunbridge Wells Museum.*

24. The work table in plate 23 with the lid open. *Tunbridge Wells Museum.*

25. Some of Robert Russell's distinctive nineteenth-century marquetry. Sometimes, as in the box at the top, he used end grain mosaic borders round a marquetry centre. *Tunbridge Wells Museum.*

26. Two elaborate desk boxes of the 1860–70 period. The one on the right, shown open, contains its original presentation card for Christmas 1865. *Pinto Collection, Birmingham Museum.*

27. The Pantiles. The picture and its frame are in Tunbridge end grain mosaic; probably by James Brown, first an apprentice of Hollamby, later a partner in Boyce, Brown & Kemp. *Pinto*

28. Fenner & Nye's masterpiece—a slice from their graduated perspective block of Battle Abbey. It may be earlier than the general run of end grain mosaic. *Pinto Collection, Birmingham Museum.*

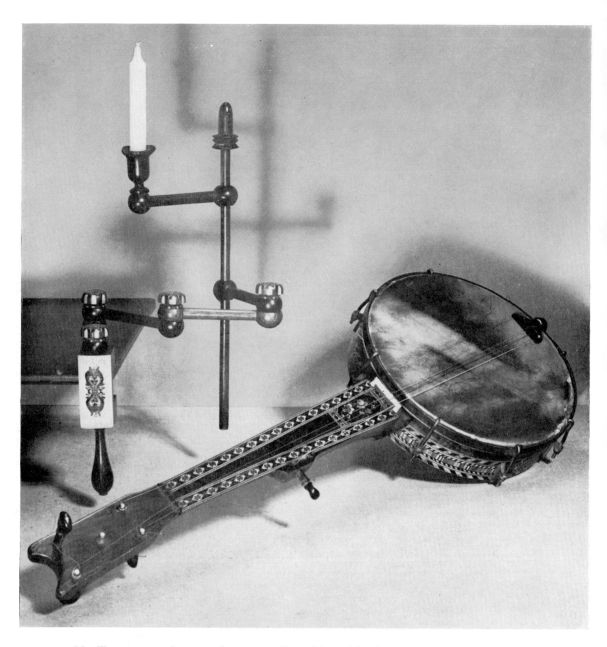

29. Two unusual examples—an adjustable table-clamping candle arm with screen holder, and a banjo. Both were probably made between 1840 and 1850, although the inlaid banding round the 'drum' of the banjo is a pattern found much earlier. The candle arm of rosewood has knuckles in stickware. *Pinto Collection, Birmingham Museum.*

an 18-in. long block produced something like 900 slices. This is just a fairy story, as it would mean an average of 50 slices to the inch: 50 slices to the inch would be a highly creditable performance for modern knife-cut veneer, whereas Tunbridge mosaic was *saw*-cut into slices which were usually $\frac{1}{16}$ in. thick, but occasionally thicker.

We have checked the facts with Mr. A. Frank Hemsley and have also carried out tests with some of the actual saws used by the mosaic workers. These saws naturally vary in thickness according to diameter—the greater the diameter, the thicker the saw. Our tests show that the thinnest saw, capable of slicing through, say, a 1-in. diameter block, wasted approximately $\frac{1}{32}$ in. in sawdust. Allowing for the thickness of the $\frac{1}{16}$ in. slice additionally, this means that 10 or 11 mosaic slices were the optimum out of each one-inch run of block. For a block, say, 3 in. or 4 in. in diameter,—a saw making a $\frac{1}{16}$ in. cut was required, so eight slices of mosaic to the inch run of block was about the average and a 6-in. diameter block might lose even more in sawdust.

Now what really was the average length of a block? Mr. Hemsley says 9 or 10 inches; most of those which we have examined were 6 in. to 8 in. long, one or two 12 in. long, but none 18 in. long, although we accept that they did exist for blocks of small diameter—those rather in the peppermint rock category.

Blocks for mosaic bandings or borders were usually assembled in approximately $3\frac{1}{2}$-in. long sections and then joined up to form pattern repeats, like the geometric banding block on the right of Plate 6. Sometimes they were strengthened by facing the block with a $\frac{1}{16}$-in. thick cross banding of veneer which, after transverse slicing, shows as a $\frac{1}{16}$-in. stringing or edging.

Gluing with hot animal glue, the only adhesive used during the mosaic and earlier periods, was a slow and messy operation. Animal glue has to be kept constantly at the right temperature for working—around 120°F. It sets by gelling and absorption of the water into the wood, but the joints do not develop much strength under twelve hours from gluing. In consequence, the gluing up of a mosaic block had to be done in stages, at least one day apart for each layer of sticks.

Using one of the assembly charts and coloured designs, as shown in Plate 4, each layer of sticks could be built up separately without a pause and the layers of edge-glued sticks could then be glued to each other on subsequent days, checking against the colour design that the layers were assembled in the correct order.

A circular block, however, such as those in Plate 6, was a more tedious affair to glue up. First, the centre sticks of the design had to be glued, strung tightly and allowed to dry. Next day, the string was removed and the next surrounding layer of sticks was glued on, strung round, and allowed to dry. These operations were repeated daily until the circumference of the bundle increased to the stage where the pattern was complete; the build-up of a large circular mosaic block could, therefore, spread over a week or two.

Circular hollow objects, such as serviette rings and some small containers, had the sticks, of contrasting colours, glued round a solid wood core, the whole or major part of which was subsequently drilled out, leaving only the circular stickware outer wall (for stickware see p. 51).

After the assembled and glued mosaic blocks had been cross saw-cut into $\frac{1}{16}$-in. thick end grain slices, the slices were glued on to the wood surface which it was desired to decorate; then they were sanded carefully and polished or varnished.

The pair of early nineteenth-century miniature tables, one shown tilted, in Plate 6, are a rare and interesting example of transitional work, 1825–30, with fine wood mosaic butterflies inserted into a conventional Tunbridge ware marquetry background of boxwood, walnut and ebony veneers. As stated in the previous chapter, mosaic birds and butterflies are said to have been introduced by James Burrows.

In the wood mosaic, colour and end grain formation were much more important than 'figure' and the ornament of most of the early pieces was geometric, partially through restriction to a comparatively small range of native woods and probably partially through lack of experience; imported woods, however, were soon (and literally) pressed into service and the increase in the range of shades and grain, coupled with advancing skill, made possible elaborate floral designs and the building and landscape pictures which became such a feature of mid- and late nineteenth-century work. At one time, chiefly between 1840 and 1860, the mosaic was used to imitate the then fashionable 'Berlin woolwork', for which, according to that authority on needlework, Miss Sylvia Groves, the use of coloured patterns, painted by hand on a network of small squares, had been devised by the German print seller, Phillipson, in 1804.

Sometimes blocks of suitable size and shape, instead of being sliced across into mosaic after assembly, were turned on a lathe; the pattern varied according to the depth of cutting on the turning tools, and this process was known as stickware. Examples of stickware, sometimes in conjunction with mosaic bandings round bases, and mosaic patterns on plinths, are shown in Plate 11. Some writers have stated that Tunbridge stickware goes back to the seventeenth century and, moreover, that this idea of gluing together into blocks, longitudinal strips of many-coloured, home-grown woods and then turning them on the lathe to show pattern, is the missing link between marquetry and the cross-sliced wood mosaic. It is a tempting theory, but we must admit that we have never seen any Tunbridge stickware which appears earlier than of nineteenth-century date, nor do we think it exists. It seems to us obvious that having once created a stick mosaic block with the pattern running right through it, the possibilities of cutting end grain slices from the block would be quite obvious and much more quickly apparent than the possibility of creating designs by profiling the block on a lathe.

Cube pattern, in which contrasting colours and figuring of *veneers* are used, is not end grain mosaic; it is a clever cutting and selection of veneers, devised to convey an impression of perspective. It was used in the late eighteenth- and early nineteenth-century Tunbridge ware, as shown in Plate 5, and also on furniture. This pattern continued in popularity and without change, as centrepieces in mosaic borders, late into the nineteenth century. Cube itself, therefore, cannot be dated, but absence of mosaic borders, or the presence of only narrow and simple geometric ones, may indicate early specimens. The two examples of boxes in the two top rows of Plate 12 date from about 1835; some of the others in the illustration were made between 1840 and 1890. The large box at the top, fitted for writing, contains ink bottles with mosaic tops. In the second row, the clothes brush and the silk-skein holder, on the right, are rather rare; the cheroot case in the same row is also a 'find'. Obelisk thermometer stands were inspired by Cleopatra's Needle, brought to London in 1878; the example illustrated, inappropriately decorated with a mosaic dog, is by Hollamby. Another dog by Hollamby is shown on a needle case in Plate 13.

Two fundamental misconceptions about Tunbridge mosaic are widely spread. One is that all early work is fine and that all late work is coarse; the other is that all early work is polished and late work varnished. Actually, all the best nineteenth- and early twentieth-century work (broadly, the mosaic period) is finely jointed and matched, whilst poorer pieces are apt to be decorated with offcuts of bandings, forming badly spaced borders, not matching at mitres. Early pieces may be french polished or finished with several coats of a good shellac varnish, well rubbed down between coats. The late varnished pieces are finished with an easily crazed spirit varnish, which shows white where scratched. Size of tesserae has no connection with fineness of jointing, but in general the most minute tesserae were used in mid- and late nineteenth-century work. Because the industry was meeting increasing competition and fighting a losing battle with machine products in the second half of the century, it is true that a larger percentage of the late mosaic is varnished than had been the case earlier. Also due to competition and the Victorian love of novelty and pictorial and romantic art, the Tunbridge makers tended to concentrate their later—that is, those of the second half of the nineteenth century—mosaic designs on castles, such as Eridge, Dover and Tonbridge, great houses, such as Knole and Penshurst Place, and ruined abbeys, such as Muckrose, and further to embellish some of their work with elaborate borders and bandings. Nevertheless, much of this late work is well designed, dignified and historically interesting. For instance, the two fitted boxes in the top row of Plate 13, both show Eridge Castle, but the one on the right, a fitted writing box by Nye, shows it with a superstructure on the tallest tower; this superstructure was demolished about 1874, after which the box on the left and the domed one, bottom right, must have been made.

In Plate 15 are examples of simple but not coarse, geometric designs, made about 1840–5. The two triple stamp boxes, second shelf up, are by Nye and Barton respectively. Penny postage, which was introduced before gummed envelopes, boosted sales of sealing wax outfits and the circular rimmed, octagonal boxes, third shelf up, resulted. They are divided inside into radiating compartments for signets, sealing wax and matches, and have strikers underneath the bases, and candle holders on their lids. They are poorly designed and seem to have provided a useful outlet for offcuts of bandings on their eight faces. Between the octagonal boxes, the nice quality, revolving 'column' thermometer, on square base and with a compass in the top, is by Barton. A stickware case, containing a compass, is right of centre on the shelf below, and on the top shelf a rare yo-yo is extreme left, and a tambour needle case extreme right.

Plate 14 shows mostly geometric designs dating from 1835 to 1850. They are complex but fine in every sense. Here also are four better quality sealing wax outfits, including front left, an octagonal ruler with cavity for wax and a signet on one end. The circular boxes, two with moulded stickware rims, are mostly for snuff and are all of excellent quality, as is also the fitted work tray, top left. The glove darning stick, in front of the work tray, with finger 'eggs' on the ends, is rare. The inkstand on the right, labelled Edmund Nye, shows just how fine the mosaic can be; measuring only $10\frac{3}{4}$ in. by $7\frac{1}{4}$ in., it is decorated with square tesserae, running 22 and 23 to the inch and contains nearly 46,000 pieces. The revolving pencil, shown standing, contains more than 1,600 tesserae, but more incredible still is the stamp box, which has Victoria's head *made in mosaic*. Even with a magnifying glass and needle point, it is almost impossible to calculate the exact number, but this normal size stamp, with 60 tesserae to the inch run, must contain at least 1,000 pieces.

Plates 16 and 17 show mainly floral mosaic, made in imitation of Berlin woolwork, between 1840 and 1860. Comparison of the nice quality inkstand, front of Plate 16, with the clothes brush, centre front of Plate 17, shows how slices of one design block could be used on different objects. The adjustable candle stand in rosewood, centre front of Plate 16, is one of a pair, a considerable rarity, made about 1845. The stationery casket on the right, also made about 1845, is the same shape as the cube pattern specimen in Plate 12. The mid-nineteenth-century, domed stationery casket, left of middle row, is a more unusual shape. The floral pattern handkerchief box, on the right, is a variant of the cube pattern specimen in Plate 12. The table for pins, centre row of Plate 17, is a good specimen by Barton; the crescent-shaped pin holder on stem and foot, in the same row, was known as an Albert. The long ruler, back of Plate 17, a good specimen, has 25 tesserae to the inch run and contains approximately 7,500 of these minute wooden squares. The circular work basket in the same plate, with Prince of Wales feathers and motto in mosaic, and the box in front of it, decorated with shamrock, thistle and rose, were probably souvenirs produced for special occasions of patriotic rejoicing. The photo frame, top centre, is of poor quality, using up unmatched offcuts of floral banding. The silk-skein holder and cribbage board, on the right, are good quality pieces, as are also the needle books at the ends of the bottom row. In front are two spectacle cases.

Tunbridge wood mosaic was used to decorate quite large objects, such as tea-poys, work tables, games tables, fire screens and, even on occasion, chairs. Both Russell and Nye showed at the Great Exhibition of 1851; Nye's exhibits were described in the *Sussex Press* of March 29, 1851, as follows:

'TUNBRIDGE WELLS'

'THE GREAT EXHIBITION. The articles prepared by Mr. Nye, Tunbridge Ware Manufacturer, for the Great Exhibition, have been on view to the public at their manufactory, Mount Ephraim, during the greater part of the past fortnight. They consist of 2 tables, a lady's work box and a book stand. One of the tables has the representation of a vessel, sailing on the ocean, which viewed at a distance is a perfect imitation of nature. It is a mosaic composed of 110,800 pieces of wood of home and foreign growth in their natural colours. The other is a chromatrope table mosaic work consisting of 129,540 pieces of wood of home and foreign growth in the natural colours. The book stand is inlaid with two butterflies, one, a mosaic, consisting of 11,000 pieces of wood in their natural colours, name Sphias Leucippe, found in parts of Africa and India; and the other butterfly is a mosaic of 13,000 pieces of wood, in their natural colours, name Vanessa Juliana from Amboyna. On the work box is the representation of part of the remains of Bayham Abbey. It is a mosaic, of 13,000 pieces of wood in their natural colours . . .'

A fine Tunbridge mosaic and inlaid marquetry games table, in the collection of Her Majesty The Queen, and now at Kensington Palace, is illustrated in Plate 19. It dates from about 1845 and was made by Fenner & Co. for the Prince Consort.

This mixing of marquetry with end grain mosaic was not unusual with furniture and the larger ware. Much more unusual is all-over *veneer mosaic* furniture, entirely made up of separate tesserae. Plates 20 and 21 show a circular table and four chairs from a suite of seven chairs (two arm), in the collection of Lord Faringdon. Every chair is veneered with a different mosaic design and all the veneers on the chairs and the table are $\frac{1}{8}$ in. thick. This striking and intricate-looking suite would have been made about 1830, so in date it is close to the introduction of end grain mosaic. It could have been the same kind of 'mosaic and inlaid wood furniture' which Fenner &

Co. were showing in Regent Street, London, seven years later, the advertisement for which we have quoted on page 36.

A mid-nineteenth-century work table that is patterned entirely in end grain mosaic of the finest quality, made by Edmund Nye, is in Tunbridge Wells Museum. It is illustrated in Plates 23 and 24. In the centre of the lid, not visible in the photograph, is a Vanessa Juliana butterfly, composed of 12,000 end grain mosaic tesserae. Another very fine mosaic work table is in Maidstone Museum.

The largest piece of furniture decorated with end grain mosaic in Tunbridge Wells Museum, is a *circa* 1870 organ, probably by Hollamby. It has a view of Penshurst on the lid.

Two unusual Tunbridge pieces are the table clamping, adjustable candle arm and the banjo, Plate 29. The pivot heads of the candle arm are stickware. The banjo has some 1840–50 'Berlin woolwork' mosaic decoration, but round the drum is an inlay, not mosaic, of red, brown, white, black and green woods, such as had been used on the ware at least fifty years earlier. The vivid green coloured wood used in this banding, and during the nineteenth century in cube pattern and for leaves of floral bandings, was largely obtained from fallen branches of oak, birch or beech trees which were in an early stage of decay through being attacked by the fungus *Chlorosplenium aeruginosum*. Contrary to what has sometimes been written, the decay did not harden, but softened the fungus-stained wood and it could only be used in the early stages of the fungal attack. When supplies of the fungal-attacked green wood no longer sufficed to meet demand, probably late in the nineteenth century, the ingenious mosaic workers found a new way of obtaining the colour they wanted. This they did by soaking satinwood in chalybeate spring water. The iron or tannin, acting on the yellow of the satinwood, produced a vivid green effect. Mr. A. Frank Hemsley recalls how, when he was a young apprentice at Boyce, Brown & Kemp in 1917, earning 7s. 6d. per week, he was sent every Saturday morning down to The Pantiles with a hand cart; he delivered finished Tunbridge mosaic to Porter's Arcade and the Post Office, two of the shops selling it, and he brought back two five-gallon drums of the chalybeate water for dying satinwood green, and some creamy white woods a grey, which as the wood has yellowed with age, have now become a browny-grey.

The woods most favoured for the grey effects were sycamore, bird's-eye maple and holly; some of the most beautiful and expensive mosaic effects were produced in this manner. Plate 22 shows a selection of this fine quality work, set against backgrounds of grey bird's-eye maple. The larger book-rest, dating from about 1840–5, is particularly handsome, being hand polished and with all edges rounded and mosaic covered, a treatment and finish only given to objects of the highest quality. The back of this rest is veneered with rosewood. Note the ribbon book marker, with four mosaic button ends.

The mosaic period, commencing just after the Regency, coincided with the zenith of the rosewood fashion for furniture; in Tunbridge mosaic, rosewood continued as the most popular background veneer for boxes up to the end of the century, which unfortunately was nearly the end of the industry also. Solid rosewood was used for Tunbridge small turnery, but for larger circles, beech cores with mosaic facings were the general choice. Small rectangular boxes are usually of mahogany, covered with mosaic inset in rosewood borders; large boxes are generally made of pine, similarly treated. First quality large boxes have, under the bases, narrow rims of veneer, forming a frame to a recessed paper panel, usually grained to simulate leather. The insides of such boxes are mostly lined with gaily patterned Regency or Victorian papers.

Holly, boiled in water to make it white, was used largely for contrasting light backgrounds to dark rosewood or ebony surrounds, particularly where it was desired to silhouette buildings, etc.—see Plates 13, 16 and 26. This combination gives a sharp black and ivory effect, as opposed to the 'Sir Walter Scott romantic' of the misty ruin of Muckrose Abbey, framed in chalybeate dyed bird's-eye maple on the box bottom left in Plate 22.

Although lignum vitae had been imported for seventeenth-century work and mahogany was widely used in the eighteenth century, the majority of Tunbridge ware inlay and the early nineteenth-century geometric mosaic was made from native woods. Robert Russell, whose distinctive work, illustrated in Plate 25, covered the first half of the nineteenth century, largely used furze and holly from Tunbridge Wells Common and, as mentioned in the previous chapter, specimens of wood which showed fine colour or interesting markings, which were brought to him by local gardeners. When elaborate floral bandings became fashionable about 1840 and when architectural, animal and landscape views were used as centres to them in the second half of the century, a wider range of colour and markings was required and some 160 to 180 varieties of wood were reputed to have been used. The names of some of these are given as white and grey holly, sycamore, laburnum, plum, oak, yew, chestnut, laurel, lilac, acacia, birch, walnut, apple, pear, tulip, kingwood, black and green ebony, palmyra, partridge, prunus, canary, bay, botany oak, beech, beef (the Botany Bay oak), fustic, orange, zebra, box, rosewood, mahogany, bird's-eye maple, purpleheart and Red Saunders or ruby wood. The Pinto Collection, Birmingham Musum, contains a large selection of short ends of exotic and rare woods from the Fenner & Nye hoard. Another interesting find in the hoard was the original Fenner & Nye boxwood gauges for drilling holes. These gauges were based on the coinage and marked on their ends, 3*d*. piece, 4*d*. piece, 6*d*. piece, shilling, florin, etc.

It is said that assembly of a fine mosaic block was sometimes delayed for months, awaiting selection of a rare coloured wood from a fresh shipment arriving in a 'tea clipper'. Then the block, if a complicated one, might take a man several weeks in sorting sticks against the colour assembly chart, before proceeding to the laborious gluing-up operation already described. As he also had to be highly skilled, with perfect eyesight and possessing infinite patience, it is not surprising that the best and most intricate work commanded high prices. It would be interesting to know the price paid for the elaborate table-desk boxes, Plate 26. That on the right, shown open, can be dated exactly, because it contains the programme of the presentation ceremony and the delightful Valentine-like, cut-card pictured, saying

'Presented to Mrs. Blakeney (wife of the Rev. R. P. Blakeney, D.D., LL.D.,) by the Misses Dickson, their pupils and Miss Gatchell in token of affectionate regard and esteem. Christmas 1865.'

A very great rarity is the beautifully made combination dial-operated sovereign box, shown assembled and taken apart, Plate 18. It is a most ingenious device, which opens only when the word SURREY is spelt downwards by rotating the rings to bring the correct letters into alignment. When this combination is effected, a vertical slot comes into line in the yew wood rings forming the inner lining of the box, and allows the ivory teeth to be withdrawn, as shown in centre. So far, we have only seen the one example of this device, which was presented to the Pinto Collection by a visitor.

A special *tour de force* of mosaic workers was a picture of The Pantiles, made of and framed in mosaic. James Brown, an apprentice of Hollamby's and later a partner in Boyce, Brown & Kemp, claimed to be the first to produce this subject, illustrated in Plate 27. Examples vary greatly in quality; this one, made about 1850, is one of the finest. The strips forming the picture run 28 to the inch, but they vary in length, making computation difficult; there are, however, some 20,000 tesserae in the frame alone, which measures $9\frac{1}{4}$ in. by $7\frac{1}{4}$ in.

Plate 28 is Fenner & Nye's masterpiece—their cutting from the block of Battle Abbey. It has been described by one writer as being 'the finest wood-craft of its kind in the world' and we think this is no exaggeration. It has also been stated that it was made between 1780 and 1790 which, if true—and we doubt it—would make it the oldest Tunbridge mosaic picture known. It is certainly made on a principle entirely different from any other examples which we have seen. All others illustrated here employ the conventional mosaic technique of using tesserae, either all the same in size, or at least all of the same width and forming pictorial silhouettes by means of contrastingly coloured rectangles. This picture defies that convention and creates what looks like a water colour in pastel shades, obtained by using the almost indefinable variations of end grain as the artist's palette of colours. Moreover, and this is the remarkable part, the *tesserae forming the stones of the abbey graduate in size, from left to right of the picture, according to the perspective*. All the accuracy of the minute detail and the softly varying colours and shadows are contained in the natural end grain. The greatest width of this outstanding pattern is $5\frac{7}{8}$ in. and the extreme height $4\frac{3}{8}$ in. It contains approximately 4,000 pieces. One wonders how many months went in this superb creation. Although several slices from this block have survived, it could never have become a commercial proposition, but it may well be the inspiration of the later Tunbridge mosaic pictures, which often show Battle Abbey composed in the orthodox mosaic manner.

We conclude this chapter with some advice to collectors. Tunbridge wood mosaic tends to be collected rather indiscriminately; it is at present obtainable at prices ranging from a few shillings to £50 or more, even excluding furniture items. Price variations seem to be based chiefly on differences of size of objects, but there are many more factors which the discriminating collector should consider, and perhaps the most important of these is condition. Wood mosaic will stand reasonable wear, but the nature of its surface decoration, consisting as it does of minute tesserae and thin veneers, demands reasonable care in handling. Pieces which have been dropped, exposed to the sun, subjected to damp, or just generally neglected, have often lost some of their tesserae. The method of manufacture makes commercial replacement of the mosaic absolutely uneconomic and even if you try to do it yourself, you will, to be successful, require infinite patience, unlimited time and very considerable skill.

Therefore, buy pieces which are as perfect as possible. Some lifting of background veneers or of large pieces of inlay or of mosaic is not serious, provided nothing is missing, as you can soon glue them down again. Do not entirely disdain damaged pieces, because some objects are much more difficult to find than others, and some designs are rare, whilst others are common. Thus, Tunbridge mosaic reticule frames, money boxes, yo-yos, musical instruments, pencils, penholders, darning eggs, spinning tops, compasses, candle arms and stands, silk-skein holders, or miniature furniture are worth buying even if slightly damaged, but handkerchief, glove, hairpin and other boxes, spectacle cases, sealing wax outfits, rulers, cribbage boards, pen stands, serviette rings, pincushion stands, photograph frames, paper knives, etc. are plentiful and you can afford to take your choice. Again, never refuse a butterfly or bird centre, such as are shown in Plates 6 and 13, as these designs are rare.

Next, there is fineness of mosaic to consider, although the most minute is not necessarily the best design; such things as good and bad matching of mitred bandings and even cutting of 'repeats of design' should not be ignored in judging quality.

Generally, design as opposed to quality is a matter of taste: simple or complex geometric, cube, 'Berlin woolwork', buildings, landscapes, animal and bird mosaics, and plain or ornate backgrounds, all have their followers.

Finally, there is finish, which has some relation to quality; bear in mind, however, that the mosaic was made after the age of wax polishing and original condition is, therefore, not so important, because french polish and varnish do not patinate. If, therefore, you come across a good piece with undamaged mosaic but scratched surface, do not hesitate to have it repolished; indeed, much which was originally varnished has been improved by stripping and polishing.

The variety of objects decorated with mosaic was vast; many were made in several shapes, sizes and qualities and probably all with more than one design of mosaic. In consequence, a collection may run into hundreds of pieces, without any duplication. For the connoisseur, some specialization either in design or objects may be advisable. As an example, it is possible to obtain more than thirty different Tunbridge ware examples of stamp boxes alone.

As a matter of interest, we quote below some mouth-watering examples of the prices at which the mosaic pieces were sold in 1920. Most of these are taken from the 1920 price list of the Tunbridge Wells Manufacturing Co. Ltd. (successors to Boyce, Brown & Kemp).

Jewel Cabinets

Cabinet of drawers	63/- ea.
Cabinet of drawers with folding doors; velvet lined tray; inlaid lid	126/- ea.

Jewel Cases

With divisions and movable Tray	105/- ea.
Velvet lined; very old and rare designs	
Larger, with inlaid cubes	126/- ea.
Various	21/- to 70/- ea.

Trinket Boxes, etc.

Tie Pin Box	2/6 ea.
Needle Box	2/6 ea.
Brooch or Stud Box	2/6 ea.
Hair pin Box	2/6 ea.
Trunk shape Box	3/6 ea.
Seal box	4/- ea.
Pin Box. Inlaid sides	4/- ea.
Button box. do.	4/6 ea.
Trinket Box (velvet lined). Inlaid sides	5/- ea.

Glove Boxes

Inlaid lid and sides; satin lined	30/- ea.
do. (larger) with half-round lid	42/- to 50/- ea.

Handkerchief Boxes

Ladies	12/6 to 25/- ea.
Gents	27/6 to 42/- ea.

Tea Caddies

Double; very rare, grey ash	84/- ea.
Double; rosewood	126/- ea.
Various	21/- to 42/- ea.

Stamp Boxes

Single. Inlaid sides	2/6 ea.
With divisions for 3 kinds	3/6 ea.

Photo Frames

Snapshot	2/- ea.
Postcard	3/6 ea.
Cabinet	10/6 ea.

Pin Cushions

Toilet Pincushion (no box)	1/6 ea.
Mounted on Box. Inlaid sides	4/6 to 6/6 ea.

Inkstands

Glass Inkwell	5/- to 10/6 ea.
Crystal glass; N.P. fittings	15/- ea.
do. with 2 stamp boxes	25/- ea.

Playing Card Boxes

Tom Thumb (two packs)	5/- ea.
One Pack. Satin lined, velvet bottom	7/6 ea.
Two packs	12/6 ea.
Bridge Box (2 packs & Score sheets)	17/6 to 50/- ea.

Cigarette Boxes

To hold about 200 with 2 divisions	30/- ea.
Ladies	5/- ea.
Various	8/6 to 21/- ea.

Book Rests

Hinged ends. Inlaid	7/6 ea.
Hinged end. Inlaid. Expanding	21/- to 42/- ea.

Cotton Boxes

Inlaid lid (loose lid)	2/6 ea.
Inlaid lid (hinged lid)	2/6 to 10/6 ea.

Book Markers and Cutters

Book markers—2 buttons	1/- ea.
do. 3 do.	1/6 ea.
do. 4 do.	2/- ea.
Book marker and Paper Cutter	2/- to 3/6 ea.
Paper Knife, steel blade, inlaid handle	5/- ea.

Miscellaneous

Kettle Holder	1/- ea.
Wax and Emery holders	1/- ea.
Needle Book	1/- ea.
Serviette Rings	1/3 ea.
Pen holders	1/6 ea.
Glove Menders	1/6 ea.
Knitting Pin Sheaths	2/- ea.
Needle Book	2/6 ea.
Pin Tray	2/6 and 4/- ea.
Cribbage Board	4/- ea.
Watch hanger and Study Tray	6/- ea.

PART TWO

SCOTTISH SOUVENIR WOODWARE

30. (*upper*): Seven finely hand-painted snuff boxes, of which six depict sporting scenes and one pictures a cock and hen. The three at the top and the one in the centre were by Smith of Mauchline, made between 1832 and 1837. *In the Collection of the Marquess of Bute.*

31. (*lower*): Six finely hand-painted snuff boxes. Top—racing scene against tartan background, made by Lammie of Cumnock. 'Highland Dancing', on the right, 'View of Craigmillar Castle', on the left, and 'Edinburgh from the Argyll Battery, Castle' bottom right, are by Smith of Mauchline, made between 1832 and 1837. 'Hunters', bottom left, is by Lammie of Cumnock and the small chequer pattern box, in the centre, made of cedar from the ruins of Nineveh, is by C. Stiven of Laurencekirk. *In the Collection of the Marquess of Bute.*

CHAPTER ONE

Origin & Early Development of Scottish Souvenir Woodware

SCOTLAND has a long record of fine craftsmanship in woodware; those peculiarly Scottish wooden drinking vessels, the bicker and the quaich, and the ogee-shaped, lignum vitae snuff box, dating from the eighteenth century and earlier, prove this. As they are found as prized possessions in many parts of the globe, it is probable that they were favoured souvenirs for travellers to take home from Scotland before the nineteenth century.

Early in the nineteenth century, the popularity of *sneeshing* or snuff taking, the vogue for things Scottish and the perfecting in Scotland of the integral wood hinge, led to a new type of wooden snuff box becoming the most popular of a wide range of useful wooden objects made as souvenirs of Scotland—and of Burns particularly. There is no reason to believe that integral wooden box hinges originated in Scotland; they have long been made in the Karelian Isthmus and we have collected several eighteenth century, or possibly earlier, snuff boxes with wooden hinges from various countries of northern Europe. These are, however, all individually hand-made, varying considerably in finish, number of knuckles and accuracy of fitting. What some ingenious Scot did was to mechanize the process, so that he not only cheapened it, but also made *every* box hinge a perfect one. Who was the mechanical genius who invented this precise method of manufacture?

The perfecting of the hinge and its first commercialization belong to the east side of Scotland; the full development of the trade belongs to the west.

The honour for the mechanical perfecting of the hinge appears to go to James Sandy, the legless, bedridden genius of Alyth, in Perthshire. Probably the man who first commercialized the hinge for snuff boxes, tea caddies, etc., was Charles Stiven of Laurencekirk, Kincardineshire, which is only some twenty miles north-east of Alyth.

Since publication of Fraser's *History of Laurencekirk* in 1880, most writers have followed each other in ascribing the invention of the hinge to Charles Stiven, who established himself as a snuff box maker in Laurencekirk in 1783. He died in 1820, and although probably the first Scottish manufacturer to use the secret hinge on a commercial scale, he was almost certainly not the inventor. Likewise, William Crawford, of Auchinleck, was not the inventor; his claim hardly seems to have arisen until the publication of Warwick's *History of Cumnock* in 1899. According to one account, Crawford invented the hinge in 1837; according to another, he copied it from a Laurencekirk box he was repairing at that date and then introduced the snuff box industry to Ayrshire. These statements disqualify Crawford as a starter in the 'hinge stakes', but they are not necessarily true, for an earlier writer, in 1845, says Crawford had introduced the hinge to Cumnock from Laurencekirk thirty years before. To make confusion worse, another writer turned Charles Stiven, who inaugurated the business in snuff boxes, tea caddies, and so on, into the legless, bedridden genius of Laurencekirk, who invented the hinge.

Sandy's obituary notice, which was published in the *Edinburgh Advertiser* for April 30, 1819, while Stiven and Crawford were still alive and able to refute the claim states: 'He was the first who made the wooden jointed snuff boxes, some of which fabricated by this self-taught artist, were purchased and sent as presents to the Royal family.' Hone, in *The Table Book*, published in 1826, gives an account of the many inventions of Sandy, including the Laurencekirk snuff box. A book on snuff taking, published in 1840, also credits Sandy with the invention and shows an engraving of him seated in his combined bed/work bench. Finally, we quote an account of the tragic life of the brave and ingenious James Sandy and of the remarkable work which he executed. It appeared in the *Dundee Advertiser* of Friday, May 21, 1819, some six weeks after his death—

'When great men (which too often means *great rogues*) die, biographers start up in every quarter to trumpet forth their virtues—if perchance they had any—to extenuate their faults, and to record, to all who are anxious to learn the important facts, that they were born in such a place, and died in such another, aged so and so. While truth is distorted to blazon forth *their* deeds, the useful but unassuming man of genius is allowed to depart unnoticed, except by his nearest neighbours and un-recorded, except in the fleeting discussions of the village ale-house. Such has been the case with James Sandy, of Alyth; a man of great but un-tutored genius in mechanics, who died there about the beginning of last month. At twelve years of age, he had the misfortune to injure one of his legs by a fall from a tree; and having the additional misfortune to apply to a quack-doctor, he entirely lost the use of it, after a confinement of some years. At this period, he set about making a violin; in which he succeeded wonderfully well considering that his only tools were a gouge and a knife. He persevered in this employment for some time; and having procured better tools, he became more perfect in his employ-ment, and finished his violins in a very neat style. He next made flutes, clarionets, bagpipes, fishing-rods, etc., in the same superior manner; every part of the work being performed by himself. He also amused himself in taming various kinds of birds, which gave rise to a report that he hatched geese by the heat of his body. * This is one of those vague reports which it behoves the candid historian to correct: for the fact is simply this,—that a gosling, which had been hatched by a hen, having been left an *orphan* at a very tender age, James took compassion on it, and reared it till it became a *perfect goose*; and it afterwards lived with him for eight or nine years, always evincing the greatest attachment to its kind protector.

One would have thought that a man who had been confined to one spot for about five years, ran very little risk of more accident to his limbs. But it happened, that one winter, when the ice on the Burn of Alyth broke up, it gorged at the Bridge; and caused the water to rise so very high as to inundate the lower part of the house where sat the unfortunate James. As he was totally unable to move, his mother en-deavoured to drag him up stairs, beyond the reach of the flood; and in

---

* This romance also occurs in the 1826 account of Sandy in Hone's *Table Book*.

the attempt, unluckily broke the sound leg. Poor James was thus rendered a complete cripple; and, during the rest of his life, he sat constantly during the day on what served him for a bed at night. Now applying himself wholly to mechanics, he made several eight-day clocks; one of which played twelve tunes on bells. He afterwards studied optics; and made several telescopes both plain and reflecting; casting and turning the brasswork, making and polishing the speculums, grinding the glasses, and wholly finished them, without any assistance; except occasionally that of a person to turn his lathe, when the work was too heavy for his hands. He made artificial teeth; and a weaver in the neighbourhood having lost his arm by a threshing-mill, James made an artificial one, jointed so that the man could continue to work at his trade. For this he received a reward of ten guineas from the Trustees for the encouragement of Arts and Manufactures. He excelled in making wooden snuffboxes, such as are made at Laurencekirk; painted and varnished them himself; constructed a most ingenious machine for cutting their hinges; made circular saws, and every other kind of tool necessary for his various occupations. He knew a little music; and could play on the violin, flute and clarionet. He made several electrical machines; was an engraver, carver, and gilder, and was armourer to the Volunteers while they continued embodied. In short, there was no piece of mechanism, however ingenious, but James Sandy could copy; and that very often in a manner superior to the original. He had a manly, expressive countenance, and was extremely civil and courteous to his visitors, among whom he could reckon most people of rank or fortune in his neighbourhood, and frequently strangers from a distance, attracted by curiosity to see so extraordinary a genius. His townspeople often intruded upon him to while away a leisure hour. The conversation was apt to get dry. Whisky was sent for to enliven it; and James sometimes partook of it to a greater extent than was good for him. He long laboured under an asthmatic complaint, which, if not brought on by his social habits, was certainly no better for them. Fancying that a more elevated situation than that which he then occupied would be favourable towards his complaint, he obtained from Lord Airly a site, on which he built a small house; and, desirous of having a trusty companion when about to remove from his old friends, he married, on the 14th March. But the last notch in James's wheel had been cut; and he was destined never to occupy his new habitation, but to exchange it for one much smaller—though large enough, withal, for the greatest king that ever existed, when obliged to doff the mockery of royalty, and to return to that dust from which he sprung. He died on the 3rd April, regretted by all that knew him, for his place will not easily be supplied. Peace to his ashes.'

The following epitaph is taken verbatim from a flat stone, about 6 ft. by 4 ft., raised 30 in. or so in height above the tomb in which his remains are placed—

To the Memory of
JAMES SANDY, Feuar in Alyth
a self-taught artist of distinguished eminence.
A few of the friends of genius have erected
this monument in testimony of their admiration
of the endowments which he possessed.
Uniting an intimate knowledge of the principles of
Natural Science with great powers of invention
and singular skill and elegance
in executing the most ingenious pieces of
mechanism.
He died 3rd April, 1819, aged 53,
having from an early period of his life been
closely confined to his couch by bodily infirmity.
In the goodness of a wise and compensating
Providence he triumphed over the disadvantage of
an apparently helpless and calamitous condition,
being blessed with a social and happy temper,
and preserving to the last
the faculties of his intelligent mind active and
unimpaired.
Materiem Suberab et Opus.

Ar. Crichton, Sculpr.

Reference occurs in Sandy's obituary to the many distinguished visitors attracted to his bedside from far and wide; it has long been thought that the idea for the hinge may have resulted from one of these contacts. Before its perfection, there was considerable difficulty in making a wood box sufficiently air-tight to keep snuff in the right condition and the majority of snuff boxes made in Great Britain were circular, lipped and unhinged. But owing to the hygroscopic nature of wood changing its dimension according to variations of moisture in the atmosphere, lids sometimes became loose and there was always the considerable risk of a snuff box lid coming off in the user's pocket, with dire consequences. Among the distinguished visitors who might have aroused the curiosity of Sandy by offering him snuff from a continental box with an integral wood hinge, must be counted some of the entourage of Tsar Alexander I, who visited the Duke of Atholl at nearby Blair Atholl in 1814. This belief has appeared in print before; it can neither be proved nor disproved, but the date appears too late for Sandy's mechanical perfecting of the hinge, which we have found, in a variably crude, hand-made form, on some eighteenth-century snuff boxes which are probably of Scottish workmanship.

We are, therefore, faced with the distinct possibility that Stiven and maybe others were making boxes by hand, with integral wood hinges, at an earlier date than is known, but there seems little doubt that Sandy perfected and mechanized the idea. As to whether Sandy sold his invention to Stiven, or whether Stiven worked out the principle independently, is unknown, but by 1819, the date of Sandy's death, the box was already being described as the Laurencekirk box.

Charles Stiven was born in the village of Drumlithie in 1753 and was a joiner on Lord Gardenstone's estate; he moved to Laurencekirk when he was thirty. He was then already established as a maker of high class snuff boxes, which at that time formed an important industry, although whether he only worked in wood is unknown. He is said to have been persuaded to move by the benevolent and eccentric Lord Gardenstone, who was a snuff addict, was Superior of the Burgh of Laurencekirk and was a very good friend to Stiven.

Stiven's premises were the stagecoach booking office, and Stiven's woodware, particularly the hand-painted, secret hinged snuff boxes, soon acquired wide approval by snuff takers passing through and stopping at Laurencekirk by the coaches. Writing about 1807, George Robertson, a farmer at Granton, near Edinburgh, has this to say about Laurencekirk, in *A General View of Kincardineshire or The Mearns*:

'Among other manufactures introduced by Lord Gardenstone, this town is still pre-eminent for making an elegant kind of wooden snuff-box, remarkable for the correctness of the hinge, and a pretty varnish. This kind of toy gives employment to two artists, who, with all their industry, are never able to furnish so fast as their orders require.'

Later in his discourse, Robertson writes:

'Laurencekirk, the next village as to population, consists rather of shopkeepers than mechanics. There is a thriving bleachfield however, in its vicinity. And one of the most elegant manufactures in Scotland is in this village, namely, that of the beautifully varnished wooden snuff-boxes, already taken notice of in a preceeding chapter. But this mystery employs only one or two artists.'

The word artist may be taken in its literal sense here, for all the early wooden snuff boxes with secret hinges, if decorated, had their lids hand-painted by artists, some of whom went on to win international renown. But we can take the origins of hand-painted woodware at Laurencekirk back another twenty years, to 1787 and give credit for the introduction of artists to that patron of art and industry, Lord Gardenstone, who had probably set Stiven up as a box maker in Laurencekirk four years earlier. The following is an extract from Lord Gardenstone's travelling memorandum of 1787—

'Arrived at Spa. I have engaged Mr. Brixhe, painter, to go to Laurence-kirk, on a plan to introduce and establish his art of painting on wood, which is elegently practised in this place. They make all sorts of trinkets, toilets, dressing boxes, tea chests, snuff boxes, pick-tooth cases, etc. etc. He is a man about thirty years of age, bred to all branches of the art, and particularly eminent for painting flower pieces, and imitations of marble chaffers. For twenty years, he has wrought with Monsieur de Lou, who gives him a great character for sobriety, as well as skill in his business. I am bound to give him thirty pounds for three years certain, and five guineas with every apprentice whom he engages to teach. During that period, his works are all at my disposal. I furnish materials; and if, at the

[71]

end of three years, he chooses to settle and carry on business for himself, I give him a commodious house for life, without rent.'

One assumes that if Brixhe had been working for twenty years with Monsieur de Lou, he was a bit more than thirty years of age.

In a footnote, Lord Gardenstone adds: 'He has since actually settled in Laurencekirk, where he is carrying on the practice of this business with great reputation, and where I made a new bargain with him.'

It will be seen, therefore, that if Stiven and Sandy both played important parts in the early stages of the Scottish snuff box production, due credit must be given to Lord Gardenstone for producing the play. We conclude this brief account of his contribution to the artistic side of the enterprise by an anecdote reported by Hone in his *Year Book* for 1832:

'Lord Gardenstone (Francis Gardner Esq.), who died in 1793, also a lord of session and author of several literary works, had strange eccentric fancies, in his mode of living; he seemed to indulge these chiefly with a view to his health, which was always that of a valetudinarian. He had a predilection for pigs. A young one took a particular fancy for his Lordship, and followed him wherever he went like a dog, reposing in the same bed. When it attained the years and size of swinehood, this was inconvenient. However, his Lordship, unwilling to part with his friend, continued to let it sleep in his bed room, and, when he undressed, laid his clothes upon the floor, as a bed to it. He said that he liked the pig, for it kept his clothes warm till the morning.'

As snuff taking declined, Stiven's firm went over more and more to tea caddies and other fitted boxes, with the same exclusive features; they continued to make these during the several generations of Stiven manufacture and, like the rival makers who sprang up, they gradually added other lines to their range. However, even though they took full advantage of every change of fashion, there was a decline in demand from about 1830 and finally, around 1868, they all ceased trading. Their workmanship was always of the highest quality from start to finish of their career. Boxes made after about 1819 are usually stamped Charles Stiven & Sons, or Stiven & Son. The son, Alexander, continued the Stiven & Son marking after his father's death. The firm were Royal Warrant Holders and the head of it is said to have had the honour of exhibiting his ware to the royal family at Balmoral on several occasions. A fine box, stamped C. Stiven, Laurencekirk, and made from various historic woods, detailed in the caption, is shown centre of Plate 35 and a box, made of the cedar from the ruins of Nineveh, centre of Plate 31, is also stamped C. Stiven, Laurencekirk.

Additional to the Stivens, at least three other snuff box makers established themselves in Laurencekirk early in the century—W. Crab, W. & G. Milner and Robert Macdonald. The last was Stiven's son-in-law, and Crab and William Milner were former apprentices. Very few boxes have come to light bearing these makers' names and it seems probable that they were never in as large a way of business as the Stivens. A green chequer pattern snuff box, stamped McDonald, Laurencekirk, is shown in Plate 32.

How the secret of the hinge travelled to Ayrshire and leaked out there, resulting in the development of a world-wide Scottish souvenir industry, is told in the next chapter.

CHAPTER TWO

The Growth of the Scottish Souvenir Industry & its Makers

AS WE HAVE SHOWN in the previous chapter, the Stiven family were facing competition in Laurencekirk, Kincardineshire, from early in the nineteenth century. Most writers, in recent years, have dated the Ayrshire discovery of the secret of the wooden hinge by William Crawford, sometimes also referred to as John or George Crawford, of Cumnock, Ayrshire as being about 1836–7. This is incorrect; Old Cumnock and the adjoining parish of Auchinleck were commencing to challenge Laurencekirk some thirty years earlier—that is, just about as soon as competition to the Stivens commenced in their home town. Lord David Stuart has brought to our notice that William Acton of Strathaven, in *General View of the Agriculture of the County of Ayr*, 1811, writes under his section on 'Manufactures':

'Snuff-boxes are made by William Crawford, in Cumnock, with a surprising degree of neatness. They are either of plane-tree or American maple. The boxes are 3 inches, or $3\frac{1}{4}$ in length, 2 inches broad, and $\frac{1}{2}$ inch deep, within, or $\frac{6}{8}$ the over. The joints or hinges of the lids are executed in a manner, that cannot be surpassed. The boxes have a slight bend, to suit the pocket, convex on the bottom, and concave on the top. Those, which are made of maple, are neatly polished without colouring; and such as are of plane-tree are painted or coloured. Egyptian, Roman or

Chinese figures, and other ingenious devices, are formed on them all, executed by the hand, with a neatness and regularity, that is truly surprising. They are handsomely tin-plated within, and sold at from one to two guineas each. Mr. Crawford has been altogether self-taught in this species of manufacture, and has brought it to a degree of perfection which cannot be surpassed.'

This is a very accurate description, except that the boxes are usually convex on the top and concave on the bottom. Top left of Plate 37 is one of the handsome burr maple boxes referred to in this description. The concave sides follow the fashion of silver snuff boxes of the same period. The natural figure of the wood forms its own ornament.

By 1825, the industry in Old Cumnock in wooden hinged snuff boxes had probably reached its zenith; the *Commercial Dictionary of Scotland*, 1825, states:

'Here those beautiful articles, known by the name of Scotch snuff-boxes, were first made; which business continues to form a valuable branch of manufacture, and is still confined to Cumnock, with one or two exceptions.'

Under 'Merchants and Tradesmen', the following are mentioned, under the heading 'Snuff-Box Makers'—

> Buchanan (a painter)
> Crawford Wm. (original maker)
> Crichton & Co.
> David Crichton
> Gibson Wm.
> Lammie Alex.
> Mitchell James

and under 'Miscellaneous'

> Paterson John, snuff box painter.

There are many, slightly varying, stories of how William Crawford came to discover the secret of the Laurencekirk wooden hinge and also how it escaped and spread to various other Ayrshire villages; basically, however, nearly all the stories agree on the salient points, which may be summed up as follows. Some time in the first decade of the nineteenth century, probably about 1806–7, Sir Alexander Boswell, the poet son of James Boswell, the biographer of Samuel Johnson, who lived at the family seat, Auchinleck House, near Old Cumnock, built by the Adam brothers, had guests staying with him. Among the guests was a Frenchman, who accidentally broke the hinge of his Laurencekirk snuff box and sent it to the village to be repaired. Other versions of the story say that (*a*) it was Sir Alexander Boswell's box and (*b*) that the box was sent to the village for refilling with snuff and that it was accidentally dropped and broken there. Anyway the box was sent for repair to Mr. Wyllie, the Old Cumnock or Auchinleck village gunsmith and watchmaker. Wyllie had an ingenious employee, William, John or George Crawford, who was employed to execute the repair. In attempting it, solder ran into the hinge joint and rendered it useless. It was impossible to melt the solder out of the joint without burning the box. After numerous experiments, Crawford succeeded in making a little instrument which neatly cut the solder out of the joint. Having successfully repaired a Laurencekirk box, it was not long before Wyllie and Crawford thought of making facsimiles and they soon devised tools and jigs to do this successfully. Wyllie and Crawford then formed a partnership and concentrated on the making of wooden snuff boxes with the secret hinge. They seem to have built up a profitable business because of the excellence of their work and the secret of the hinge, but after twelve years they quarrelled and Crawford moved to the neighbouring parish of Cumnock (New), there setting up a rival establishment. At first it seems to have been a very high grade and successful business; Crawford, according to some accounts, was employing such up-and-coming artists as Daniel Macnee, Horatio M'Culloch and William Leighton Leitch to hand-paint pictures on the box lids; according to other accounts, Macnee worked for Adam Crichton. The box, top of colour Plate 31, a racing scene against a tartan background, was made by Lammie of Cumnock and has a note inside in the writing of the 4th Marquess of Bute, saying 'Painted by Sir Daniel Macnee and W. L. Leitch'. As will be seen in Chapter 4, Leitch also worked for Smith of Mauchline.

After a time, the secret of the invisible hinge escaped once more, some say via a tool-maker employed by Crawford. But however it occurred, it was a big leak this time, one which could not be stopped, and it was not long before ex-employees of Crawford and of Wyllie were going into the wood hinged box business on their own account in Auchinleck, Old and New Cumnock, and nearby Catrine, Ochiltree and Mauchline.

Whilst we have never seen a complete hinge cutting machine, we have a set of cutters and also some of the blanks from which the cutters were made. These particular ones were used by the Smith family at Mauchline. Whether they are identical with the ones which Sandy, Stiven, Crawford or some of the other makers devised, we do not know, but they clearly show their watchmaking ancestry and a watchmaker friend has shown us how they may have been used to cut and fit the wooden hinge knuckles. They consist of a range of serrated cutters like watch pinions, designed for use at varying angles, some sharpened to cut on their end faces, some on their radii and others at angles in between. After the knuckles were cut, fitted and drilled through, a brass pin was inserted. This pin was cut $\frac{1}{4}$ in. shorter than the length of the box and a $\frac{1}{8}$-in. long sycamore plug was inserted and glued in at each end, imprisoning and entirely concealing the ends of the pin.

The following is a slightly different version of how the secret of the hinge leaked out. It is taken from the *Art Journal* of 1850 and it has an air of authenticity and fills in some of the gaps in the account already given:

‘The objects of ornamental wood-work, for which this manufactory is celebrated, originated in the making of snuffboxes, at the village of Lawrencekirk, in the north of Scotland. These boxes, from the great beauty of the hinge, soon acquired considerable celebrity, and one of them falling into the hands of the late Wm. Crawford, of Cumnock, in Ayrshire, a very clever and ingenious man, he immediately applied himself to produce a similar box, but found he was greatly at a loss for the mechanical apparatus with which the *hinge* was made; he persevered however, and ultimately discovered a method of making the hinge, entirely different from that pursued by the Lawrencekirk makers, but equally effective. For many years Mr. Crawford managed to keep his secret, and thereby obtained very high prices for his snuffboxes; he employed a gunsmith in the neighbouring village of Auchinleck, to construct his tools for making the hinge; ultimately, Mr. Crawford, from

some circumstance or other, took up a suspicion (which proved ground-
less) that the gunsmith had exposed his secret; being a man of rather
dogmatic temper, he went to a clock-maker in Douglas, (a distance of
nearly thirty miles, where he was unknown) and employed him to make
these secret tools; he did so, without having the least idea of the purpose
for which they were intended. It happened, however, that in course of
a short time, the Douglas clock-maker's apprentice, Archibald Sliman,
came to commence business in Cumnock, where he soon met Mr.
Crawford, for whom he had made the little mysterious tools, and learn-
ing the celebrity of his snuffboxes, he at once saw the mode in which they
were applied to the making of the hinge. Sliman at once entered into a
partnership with a carpenter of the name of Adam Crichton, and commenced snuffbox making; the tools for the hinge were to be produced by
Sliman, and as an equivalent, Crichton was to provide the wood, and do
the carpenter's work of a new house for Sliman. When Sliman produced
the hinge tools, in a small piece of paper which scarcely occupied the
hollow of his hand, Crichton thought himself cheated. A violent alter-
cation ensued, and they began manufacturing snuffboxes separately.
Very soon several other people began making them, so that in course of
a few years—say about 1820—the manufacturing of snuffboxes alone was
supposed to bring eight or ten thousand pounds yearly into the small
village of Cumnock.'

Once the secret of the hinge was known to a number of people, price
cutting of the snuff boxes followed quickly. This led to the creation of a vast
range of different products, each maker naturally trying to keep ahead of his
rivals in marketing of novelties, each of which at first would command
good prices. A description of the eventual range of goods manufactured is
rather anticipating the future of the story, but this seems the place to insert
an account of the snuff box manufacture as the Rev. Ninian Bannatyne
saw it in 1837. It is taken from his *New Statistical Account, Parish of Old
Cumnock*. He records the growth of Cumnock on account of the snuff box
trade and weaving and then, under the heading 'Manufactures', writes:

'Cumnock has long been famed for the ingenious and beautiful manufacture of wooden snuff-boxes, which has been carried on in it, for the

last thirty years.* It rose from a very small and rude beginning to its present state of perfection. An ingenious artist of the name of Crawford caught the first idea of them from a box made at Laurencekirk, which had been sent to him to repair. The distinguishing excellence of the Cumnock snuff-boxes lies in the hinge, which is extremely ingenious in point of contrivance, as well as exquisitely delicate in point of execution; so that it is with much propriety styled "the invisible wooden hinge". The principle on which the hinge is formed, as well as the instruments employed in making it, were for many years kept a secret; but are now no longer so. The wood used in the manufacture is plane tree, it being preferable to all others by reason of its close texture. The tree is first of all cut from the centre towards the circumference into triangular pieces. These are then put to dry, and season, for at least five months, under cover. One set of artists make the boxes, another paint those beautiful designs that embellish the lids, while women and children are employed in varnishing and polishing them. The process of varnishing a single box takes from three to six weeks. Spirit varnish takes three weeks, and requires about thirty coats; while copal varnish, which is now mostly used, takes six weeks, and requires about fifteen coats to complete the process. When the process of varnishing is finished, the surface is polished with ground flint; and then the box is ready for the market.

These ingenious and elegant specimens of art have been brought by successive improvement to an astonishing degree of perfection; and the skill of the artists, sharpened and stimulated by keen rivalry, is continually advancing this curious and beautiful manufacture to a high pitch of improvement. At one time, a single box, without either painting or varnishing, but just as it came from the hands of the maker, sold for 30s., whereas at present seven such boxes can be had for 12s. A few years ago, a solid foot of wood that cost only 3s., could be manufactured into

---

* This would place the Sir Alexander Boswell snuff box episode as about 1807. The Rev. John Warrick, MA, in his *History of Old Cumnock*, written in 1899, says of the box manufacture that it '. . . began in a very small way about the year 1800 . . . Its greatest prosperity was between 1820 and 1830. After that period it gradually died away.' By the time the Rev. Bannatyne was writing, the decline had already commenced.

boxes worth £100 sterling. And then the workmanship increased the original value of the wood nearly 700 times. But at present, a solid foot of wood will only yield in finished boxes about £9 sterling. The workmanship thus only brings at present one-eleventh part of its former price.

In consequence of this great decline in the price of the boxes, the wages of the artists have also been much lowered. A few years ago, the box-maker made £1. 1s. a week, the painter £2. 2s., the varnisher 12s.; whereas now the box-maker only makes 10s. to 12s., the painter 15s., and the varnisher 5s. to 6s. a week.

A system of chequering has now almost superseded the painting of the boxes. It is done by very ingenious and nicely adjusted machines, that are worked by boys, and is much less expensive than painting. Ingenuity creates endless and ever increasing varieties of cheques; and many of them are most beautiful in point of pattern and figure, as well as of the most exquisite delicacy in point of colouring.

The yearly value of the boxes made in Cumnock may average about £1600 sterling; while fifteen years ago, the same number of boxes would have brought £6000 sterling. The total number of persons employed in this manufacture is about 50. The period of work is eleven hours a day.'

The Rev. Bannatyne's description of the sequence of operations in the seasoning of the timber and the making and decorating of the boxes is concise and excellent and the high prices obtained for the boxes in the early days were doubtless accurate, being confirmed by other writers. The Rev. Warrick says that the best hand-painted snuff boxes fetched as much as £6 or £7. He adds that

'A log of plane tree, purchased for twenty-five shillings, was calculated by the purchaser, in 1825, to be sufficient to make £3000 worth of snuff-boxes (Chambers, *Picture of Scotland*, Vol. I, p. 322).

High wages went with good trade. From 1820 to 1830, a box-maker could easily earn £1. 1s. a week, a very large wage at that time. The scene-painter could earn £2. 2s., and the varnisher 12s. After 1830 the wages went gradually down, till only about half the amount mentioned could be made. The cause of the decrease of prosperity is quite manifest. A great social custom, long adopted by the male portion of the population, was dying out. Men were ceasing to snuff, and therefore they ceased to

32. Selection of Smith's tartan ware. *Pinto Collection, Birmingham Museum.*

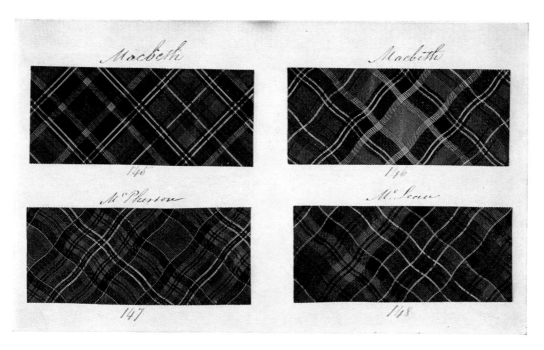

33. Selection of tartans from Smith's album of designs. *In the Collection of Lord David Stuart.*

34. Fine, hand-decorated snuff boxes. Early portrait of Queen Victoria; this is one of the 'Queen's Boxes', made by Smith of Mauchline, commencing in 1841. *Below:* Robert Burns courting Highland Mary, with quotation below 'As underneath its fragrant shade, I clasp'd her to my bosom'; on the back, the legend 'Part of the thorn under which Burns and Highland Mary had many a happy interview'.—No maker's name. *In the Collection of Lord David Stuart.*

35. Fine, hand-decorated snuff boxes. *Top:* Four-compartment box—no maker's name. *Left:* Coaching scene—no maker's name. Horse and rider—made by Murdoch of Cumnock. *Right:* Drawing of statue of a classical figure on horseback, with the words 'The Glorious Memory' above and 'No Surrender' below—made by Smith of Mauchline, Manufacturers to His Majesty (after 1832). 'Scotch Washing' by Cameron & Smith, Mauchline (Royal Arms). *Bottom:* Portrait of Sir Walter Scott and his dog—no maker's name. Tam O' Shanter and Souter Johnny, made by J. & G. McKie of Auchinleck. *Centre:* Box of various woods, inscribed—'Goldsmith's Thorn'; 'Oak of Lord Nelson Flagship Victory'; 'Oak of Holyrood Palace'; 'Oak of Airly Castle'; 'Oak of Ship which brought over King William the 3 in 1688'; 'Oak of York Minster'; 'Oak of John Knox's House'; 'Queen Mary's Yew'; 'Oak of Dunnotter Castle'; 'Torwood Oak'; 'Oak of Oldham Cathedral'; 'Oak of the Piles of London Bridge'; 'Oak of Glasgow Cathedral'; 'Oak of Elgin Cathedral'; 'Birk of Invermay'.—Made by C. Stiven of Laurencekirk.
In the Collection of the Marquess of Bute.

36. Fine, hand-decorated snuff boxes. *Top row:* The Bute Arms, with motto below '*Avito viret honore*'—no maker's name. Picture of the blacksmith's forge—no maker's name. *Centre row:* Three men drinking, with below the words 'It is the moon, I ken her horn'—no maker's name. The Jolly Beggars, made by Crawford of Cumnock. Phaeton with driver and passenger—no maker's name. *Bottom:* A hound—no maker's name. *In the Collection of the Marquess of Bute.*

37. Fine quality snuff boxes, all but one hand decorated. *Top left:* Maple burr box, the silver plaque inscribed 'George Alexander from I.P.M., 12th Oct. 1861'.— Made by C. Stiven & Sons of Laurencekirk, Makers to Her Majesty. *Top right:* A red pen-and-ink patterned box, probably by the same maker as the tea chest, Plate 39. *Left:* Hunting scene, made by Crichton of Cumnock. Arabic design box by unknown maker; this may not be Scottish, as it has a silver hinge. *Right:* Hunting scene—no maker's name. Tam O'Shanter with Souter John—maker's name indecipherable. *Centre:* Cutty Sark, and *below,* 'War'. *Pinto Collection, Birmingham Museum.*

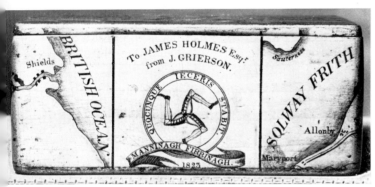

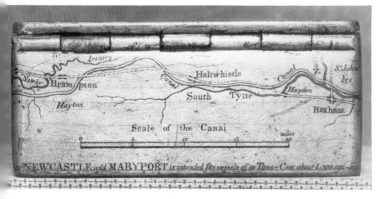

8. The top, bottom, front and back of the Solway, pen-and-ink
ecorated table snuff box of 1823. For further details, see text.
Pinto Collection, Birmingham Museum.

39. A fine quality, pen-and-ink and hand-painted three-caddy tea chest in sycamore, probably by G. Meekison of Montrose. For further details, see text. *Pinto Collection, Birmingham Museum.*

40. Selection of tartan ware by Smith of Mauchline, probably all 1840–50. The calendar was designed for the French market, for the days of the week and the months are in French. The book cover has a machine coloured picture. The lady's companion was a popular line. In front, spectacle case, pencil and parasol handle.
Pinto Collection, Birmingham Museum.

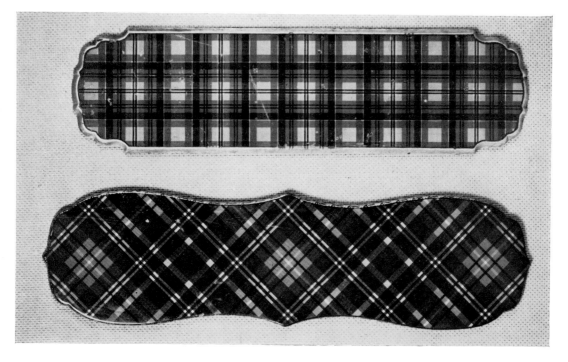

41. Examples of gilt bevel edged, tartan finger plates by Smith of Mauchline. 1840–50. *Pinto Collection, Birmingham Museum.*

42. Smith of Mauchline, razor strop in sycamore. An early example of transfer ware, hand polished and bearing the Royal Arms of William IV. Made between 1832 and 1837. *Below; detail of the Royal Arms.* *Pinto Collection, Birmingham Museum.*

43. Album of *Views of Sycamore Work*, used by one of Smith's travellers. *Collection of Timothy Trace, Esq., U.S.A.*

44. *Centre, bottom:* Paper-covered knick-knack box of unknown manufacture commemorating Queen Victoria's 1887 Jubilee, with views of Balmoral and Windsor. Selection of Smith's sycamore transfer ware comprising—*Top row:* darning block, wool ball holder, 'plane' match box holder, cheroot case. *Middle row:* whist marker, spectacle case, folding letter rack, 'bell' tape measure, perpetual calendar, card case. *Bottom row:* 'bathing machine' trinket box, egg timer, Clark's cotton box decorated with 'Fiery Cross' episode from Scott's *Lady of the Lake*, pincushion, card case. *Pinto Collection, Birmingham Museum.*

45. Smith's fern pattern ware—early twentieth century. Match holder and tea caddy in direct applied fern process; needle case with fern label on tartan background. *Pinto Collection, Birmingham Museum.*

46. Deeply carved sycamore, 'Burns', table snuff boxes; said to have been made by a blind Scotsman in Glasgow, about 1850. *Pinto Collection, Birmingham Museum.*

47. A receipt from William Leitch for an advance by Smith, dated June 2nd 1828. It states 'I have received from you this day Three pounds sterling which I agree to repay to you by allowing you to keep in your hands Thirty shillings off my next months pay and thirty . . . from the month following.'

48. Andrew Smith, aged 69, with grandson. Photograph of 1850.

49. The bust D, in Plate 51, shown here in greater detail. Probably an umbrella or parasol handle.

need snuff-boxes. An interesting book could be written on the effect of fashion and the change of custom upon trade. Not the least interesting chapter would be the extinction of the snuff-box industry, owing to the people giving up the habit of snuffing. In 1825 the value of the boxes sent out was £6000; in 1837 it was only £1600.'

The wood mostly used in Scotland, and referred to there as plane, is not the London plane, but the tree which in England is known as sycamore. It grows to perfection in the British Isles, and when cut is a beautiful creamy-white coloured wood, close textured, remarkably free from blemishes and very stable when seasoned. It darkens somewhat after exposure to the air, and by the time it was multi-coated with the varnish then used, it attained a yellow colour.

At the height of the prosperity of the industry in hand-painted, secret-hinged snuff boxes which, as the Rev. Warrick says, occurred between 1820 and 1830, there were some fifty specialist box makers in Scotland. The following list of 57 names is compiled from old records and from stamps and labels which are sometimes found in snuff boxes.

Auchinleck
Chalmers
Findlay
Gibson (?)
Johnston, W.
Macgregor, James
McKie, J. & G.
Millar, S.
Murdock
Scott, John

Bonnington
Sinclair, Geo.

Catrine
Clark, John
Kay or Kerg, Hugh
Morrison, William
Sliman, George

Cumnock
Buchanan, George
Crawford, George
Crawford, William
Crichton, Adam
Crichton & Co.
Crichton, David
Crichton, Peter
Drummond, James
Dunlop
Gibson, William
Ingram & Co.
Johnston, William & Sons
Lammie, Alex.
McCallam
Mirag (?), H.
Mitchell, James

Murdoch, H.
Samsen & Co.
Stiven

Helensburgh
Craig, Daniel or David

Laurencekirk
Crab, W.
Macdonald, Robert
Milne, W. &. G.
Stiven, Charles, & Son

Mauchline
Black & Co.
Brown, R.
Cameron
Cameron & Smith

Mauchline (cont.)
Clark, Davidson & Co.
  (George Clark,
  John Davidson)
Davidson, Wilson
  & Amphlet
Paterson
Smith, Andrew
Smith, W. &. A.

Smith, William
Wilson & Amphlet
Wilson & Co.

Montrose
G. Meekison

Ochiltree
Kay, Hugh
Murdoch

Murdoch, A., & Co. (?)
Pedon, Mungo

Unplaced
Cowan
Murdoch, D.

The list may not be complete, but probably it also contains some duplications, due to changes in names of partnerships, or to successive generations with the same surnames but different initials, carrying on the same business.

As regards the miniature painters who decorated the boxes, the most eminent were probably Daniel Macnee, William Leighton Leitch and Horatio M'Culloch, already mentioned. Additional names which have been recorded are Robert Brown, Alex Buchanan, John Paterson, John MacKinnen, Sawneg Templeton and John Anderson. As few of them ever signed or initialled their work, it is almost impossible to identify or relate it to boxes bearing makers' names or stamps. It is also difficult to ascertain how many, if indeed any, of the artists were tied to a particular box maker. Probably the majority, who only worked on boxes as a brief stage in their careers, were free-lance. Leitch worked for the Smiths of Mauchline; some of his bills have survived and a receipt for an advance, dated June 2nd, 1828, is reproduced here, Plate 47. He is also known to have painted for some of the Cumnock makers. Robert Brown also worked for the Smiths, but may have received commissions from other makers in the adjacent Ayrshire villages. Macnee probably worked for Crawford, Lammie and the Crichtons. Quoting from *History of Old Cumnock* again, the Rev. Warrick says:

'It was only to be expected that the high wages received by the miniature painters would attract young men with artistic skill from other parts of the country. This actually took place. Three artists were here for a time, who afterwards rose to great fame.

The first of them was destined to reach the highest place of honour in the world of Scottish art. His name was Daniel Macnee. At the age of nineteen, he came to Cumnock as an apprentice in Adam Crichton's boxwork, but he did not remain long. . . . One, who still remembers the young lad going to and from his work, remarked, in his quiet, pawky way, some time ago, "Ay, Macnee had a great name in Edinburgh by and by, but when he was here he was na muckle thocht o'." The humour of this we can all appreciate, and doubtless there were some engaged in box-painting along with him, who failed to detect the genius and the fineness of touch, which are certain to have distinguished even the early productions of one of the greatest portrait-painters of our time.

A curious incident is told regarding a piece of Macnee's Cumnock work. One evening, long after he had risen to fame, he was dining at Ballochmyle House. The conversation turned on Ayrshire scenery. Macnee, who said he had not seen much of it, referred to one scene of great beauty with which he had been impressed, and which he had sketched as a lad in order to paint it on a snuff-box, about to be presented to a young man leaving for South America. One of the guests immediately handed his snuff-box to the great painter, who, looking at it with surprise, remarked, "That's the very box." "And I," said the other, "am the young man." The owner of the box, which thus was seen again by the artist after a lapse of forty years, was the late Dr. Ranken of Demerara, whose representatives in Ayr still possess it. . . .

The second distinguished artist, who worked in Cumnock, was Horatio M'Culloch, so deservedly noted for his Highland landscapes. No reminiscence of his stay, however, seems to linger in the town. The fact only is certain that he served here for some time, trying his "prentice han' " in one of our local box-works.

The third was William Leighton Leitch, who became a water-colour painter of the greatest eminence. His stay in Cumnock is still remembered by old residents. The story of his struggle with adverse circumstances, till he reached his position of honour and fame, is so full of interest, that it may be briefly told as a stimulus to others. It is recorded at length in a small volume by Mr. MacGeorge of Glasgow, published in 1884, and dedicated to Queen Victoria:

"Coming home one afternoon from his work (of scene-painting)," says his biographer, "he met a young artist friend, who told him that several of his early associates, including Macnee and Horatio

M'Culloch, had gone to Cumnock, in Ayrshire, and had there found employment in painting snuff-boxes . . . and he strongly advised Leitch to go there also. This, after consulting his friends, he resolved to do. He first went by himself, and soon Mrs. Leitch joined him with their baby daughter. From working on a scale so large as the painting of scenes for a theatre, to the very minute work of snuff-box painting was a great change, but he very soon got in the way of it, and easily found employment. It was often difficult, however, to get payment for his work, and he and his young wife underwent at this time some hard trials. For about a year he worked for the general trade in Cumnock, finding employment from different dealers, when Mr. Smith, the head of a large establishment in Mauchline, having discovered his superior talent, engaged him to superintend his painting-department, and here he did some beautiful work in box-painting.''

After spending some time in Mauchline, Leitch proceeded to London . . .'.

Although the perfecting of the secret hinge in Kincardineshire, and the rediscovery of how to make it in Ayrshire, was the work of clever mechanics skilled in watchmaking, the majority of the actual workers engaged on the making were essentially woodworkers. It seems probable that a number of established turners and makers of eating, kitchen and dairy treen were among those who took up snuff box making, once they had learned about the hinge. This is borne out by the fact that nearly all the early makers also produced Scottish toddy ladles. Incidentally, Scottish toddy ladles have the stems threaded into the bowls, whilst English specimens, like spoons, are made in one piece. Changes in fashion have always been the curse of manufacturers. The men who had made quaichs and bickers (Scottish wooden drinking vessels) in the eighteenth century, doubtless also made the toddy ladles. As the specialized wooden drinking vessels were superseded by other materials, they badly needed new lines, such as the wood hinged snuff boxes, particularly as the demand for wooden toddy ladles was also dying. In retrospect, we can see that the expensive wood hinged snuff box with hand-painted picture on the lid, was also destined to have a comparatively short run, so those who made them soon made tea caddies and visiting card cases as well. It has often been written that Queen Victoria killed the custom of snuff taking; it is not true. In the *History of Old Cumnock*, already quoted, the Rev. Warrick says that in 1837, the year Victoria came to the throne, the value of the snuff boxes sent out had declined to £1,600, from £6,000 in 1825. So although snuffing continued among poorer people, it was already on the way out with the fashionable. Cigar smoking commenced to supersede it after 1815 and went on increasing throughout Victoria's reign, despite her disapproval of the habit. Cigar smoking caused the early makers to design high quality cigar magazines (cases), but this was probably the last luxury line which they produced in the hand-decorated grade. From about 1825, they were experimenting with what they called chequer designs, which developed into tartan ware and it was during the period 1825–45 that the now less expensive, but still well-finished range of goods manufactured proliferated so vastly, whilst the prices gradually reduced to starvation point. Those makers who could not keep pace with the demand for novelties and could not adapt themselves to the cheaper, semi-mechanical finishes dropped out first; by 1845, there were hardly any left except that remarkable family, the Smiths of Mauchline, who went on wrestling with fate for another century. As they made everything in the way of souvenir woodware that any other Scottish firm did, and a great deal more besides, the full range of articles and the varied finishes are detailed in the next chapter.

CHAPTER THREE

The Range of Scottish Souvenir
Woodware

THE RANGE of Scottish souvenir woodware commenced in a very modest way. The range was virtually two items—snuff boxes and tea caddies. Both were of the highest quality, fitted with the secret wooden hinge and skilfully decorated with fine hand-painted pictures and pen-and-ink work. Some hand-decorated snuff boxes are illustrated in colour Plates 30 and 31, and in Plates 34–38. An outstanding tea caddy of this early nineteenth-century period is shown in Plate 39. It dates from about 1800–10, bears no maker's stamp and is decorated both inside and out with pen-and-ink and brush work of the highest quality. Both the chest, which is 12 in. long, 6 in. wide and $5\frac{1}{2}$ in. deep, and the interior caddies are fitted with the integral hinge. On the outside of the lid of the chest is a good pastoral picture in black pen-work; inside the lid, roses are painted in natural colours. The exteriors of the chest and the caddies are decorated with an all-over network of fine red pen lines, in a black pen border, on the natural wood. The cleverness of the design, when added to the accuracy of their fitting, makes the hinge lines of the caddies invisible. A snuff box of the same design, and probably by the same maker, is shown top right of Plate 37. Another oval snuff box decorated in pen-and-ink work of the same design has recently been purchased by Mr. Peter Klein of the Birmingham Museum. As Mr. Klein's box is stamped inside with the name G. Meekison, Montrose, it seems

[86]

reasonable to assume that the two examples illustrated are by this same, hitherto unrecorded maker; it has been established that he was a boxmaker in the High Street, Montrose, in 1832, but he may have been working earlier and later.

These high quality, hand-decorated snuff boxes and tea caddies were naturally very expensive and were soon challenged by other and cheaper products. Moreover, after 150 years or more of being a social custom, snuffing was waning greatly, although it never entirely died out. The makers were, therefore, confronted between 1810 and 1820 with the necessity of increasing their range of products and simultaneously cheapening their methods of production.

The first big break through occurred with chequer and tartan ware, which was made in a wide range of objects from about 1820. Even while this was still selling well, however, although at increasingly cut prices, the Smith family of Mauchline, seeing the red light, kept a move ahead by mechanizing the tartan ware and, at the same time, developing successors in Scoto-Russian niello and in their transfer ware. Whilst the yellow finish of the varnished sycamore, in the case of transfer ware, is distasteful to many people, all the products were well made and cleanly finished and the transfer applied pictures were mostly made from splendid engraved plates, which produced much of the glamour of the old pen-and-ink picture work, at a price which a large public could afford to pay. By the time that the other makers had awakened to the fact that tartan ware was on the way out, the Smiths had travelled far on their way to encircling the globe with their new, inexpensive and much augmented range of transfer novelties; the history of transfer ware is, therefore, very much the history of the Smiths of Mauchline and is given in the next chapter.

The list of objects which now follows covers most of the objects made by the makers of transfer ware. About half the objects were also made in tartan and chequer ware, and a few in imitation niello and fern patterns, but collectors will find little beyond snuff boxes and tea caddies in the earlier and always much more expensive hand-decorated work.

Albums—photograph	Blotter cases or books	Bodkin cases
Bezique markers	Blotters, hand	Book boxes

Book covers—Bible,
psalms, hymns,
Scott's and Burns'
poems, etc.
Book markers
Bottle cases
Bottle coasters
Boxes, cylindric
Boxes for photographs
Boxes—round, square,
oblong, oval, fancy
Brooches
Brushes, clothes
Brushes, hair
Buttons, Breadalbane
Cake baskets
Calendars, perpetual
Candlesticks (Brighton
bun type)
Card (visiting) cases
Card (visiting) trays
Cauldrons (miniature)
Cheroot cases
Chests of drawers
(miniature)
Cigar cases
(magazines)
Cold cream boxes
Cotton boxes
Court plaister cases
Counter boxes
Crochet hook cases
Darning blocks
Darning eggs
Darning mushrooms
Egg cups

Egg cup stands
Egg timers
Étuis
Finger plates
Fruit knives
Glove boxes
Glove stretchers
Hair tidies
Hairpin boxes
Handkerchief boxes
Hearth brushes
Inkstands—several
novelty shapes
Jewel caskets
Knick-knack boxes
Knick-knack cases
Knitting needle cases
Knitting needle
protectors
Ladies' companions
Lancet cases
Letter racks
Lip salve cases
Match boxes, pocket
Match containers—
various novelty
types
Match stands
Medicine glass cases
Memorandum tablets
Money boxes—various
novelty shapes
Needle books
Needle cases
(knife-box type)
Needle cases advertis-

ing Singer Sewing
Machines
Notebooks
Indiarubber holders
Paper knives
Paper racks
Paper weights
Parasol handles
Pen holders
Pen trays
Pen wipers—spring
and other types
Pencils, revolving
Photograph albums
Photograph boxes
Photograph frames
Pin discs
Pin poppets
Pin trays
Pincushions—various
types
Plaster (sticking)
cases
Playing card
containers
Pomatum bottle cases
Purses
Quaichs
Razor strops and hones
Ring boxes—single
and multiple
Rouge pots
Rulers
Scent bottle cases
Scissors boxes
Serviette rings

Silk winders
Skipping rope handles
Smelling salts bottle
  cases
Snuff boxes
Spectacle cases
Spill vases
Sprinkler eggs
Stamp boxes
String boxes
Tape measure holders
  and caskets—
  various novelty
  types

Tatting shuttles
Tea caddies
Thermometer cases
Thermometer stands
Thimble cases
Thread barrels—
  including for
  Clark's and Coat's
Thread waxers
Tooth powder boxes
Toothpick cases
Trinket boxes
Vases—beaker
Vases—bucket

Vases—various
  ornamental
Watch stands—fixed
  and folding
Wax taper boxes
Whist markers
Wool ball holders
Work boxes

It will be found interesting to compare the Scottish range of products with the Tunbridge range listed in Part I, Chapter 2.

Additional to the large variety of flush, surface decorated woodware which has been described, collectors may come across some carved table snuff boxes. These all bear a family resemblance to each other and are deeply carved on all faces with scenes from the adventures of Tam O' Shanter, or shepherds and dogs. Although crude and clumsy, they are not devoid of charm. According to manuscript labels pasted in two of them, they were the work of a blind man, working in Glasgow, about 1850. Each box is hollowed out of a solid block of sycamore, with an integral hinged lid, made by hand; because iron pins were used, which have rusted in, the hinges are usually broken. Two examples are illustrated in Plate 46.

CHAPTER FOUR

The Smiths of Mauchline
& their Contemporaries

OUR RESEARCH into the history of the Smiths of Mauchline has been spread over many years. That we are able to give such a full account is due not only to persistent following up of clues, even the most slender, but also to much good fortune and curious coincidences. In telling the story of the Smith family, we shall, therefore, endeavour to include some account of the chain of singular events which led to our unravelling of the history.

At the end of the eighteenth century, Mr. Smith of Mauchline carried on the business of stone mason and achieved some local fame as a carver of gravestones. He also leased the 'hone' stone quarry at Stair and manufactured Water of Ayr razor hones. His sons William (1795–1847) and Andrew (1797–1869), who, in the absence of any evidence to the contrary, were the founders of W. & A. Smith, were trading at Mauchline in 1823; Andrew is said to have commenced in 1821. They were the youngest of a family of five. It is not known whether an earlier generation founded the Smith woodworking business at Mauchline. The name John Smith was stamped inside some snuff boxes shown at an Edinburgh exhibition in 1959. John, born 1789, and James, 1787, were older brothers of William and Andrew, so one account which says that the family business commenced round about 1810, may well be correct.

The names William and Andrew were recurrent in the Smith family. Andrew had seven children of whom two, William (II), born 1827, died 1867, known in the family as Willie, and his sister Jane came into the business. Some of the others may have done so also, but we have no record. William (II) had a son, William (III), who was born in 1863, four years before his father's early death. A Mr. McQueen carried on the business until he grew up. William (III), who remained a bachelor, then ran it until two years before the final closure in 1939; he died as recently as 1949, at the age of 86.

In 1843, William (I) and Andrew had one of their frequent quarrels, dissolved their partnership and set up separate establishments. This is the reason for some woodware being stamped W. Smith, and some A. Smith. In 1849, following William's death in 1847, Andrew revived the title W. & A. Smith, with his son William (II) as partner.

Other Makers

During the early years of the Smith partnership, their principal competitors in Mauchline, Cumnock, Auchinleck and Catrine were the firms listed in Part II, Chapter 2. Most of these firms pinned their faith too much to snuff boxes and did not diversify their range sufficiently; consequently, when snuff taking declined in popularity, they gradually went out of business. Their demise was doubtless hastened by the fact that the woodware industry was, throughout the nineteenth century, meeting rapidly increasing competition from mass-produced souvenirs made from other materials. This competition the Smiths long fought by their inventiveness and ingenuity in designing brilliant machines for combining operations, and by producing new ranges of goods in novel forms and with entirely fresh finishes.

At the exhibition held in Edinburgh in 1959, names other than those listed in Chapter 2 have been recorded stamped inside boxes, etc. These are not necessarily names of long forgotten firms: we have evidence that some of the individual craftsmen, with understandable pride, stamped their own names in the boxes sold by their employers.

The Hinge—and the Strop

Andrew, in his youth, is known to have worked in the hone business and his changeover from stone to wood working was probably via the hone, for as a companion the hone needed a strop or strap and the strap needed a wooden handle and backing. Whether Andrew and William discovered the secret of the box hinge as early as they commenced making their strops is unknown, but they seem to have had no opposition to their strops, which they continued to make for many years. Although the sale of their strops may have gradually decreased, they probably went on selling until the hollow ground 'cut-throat' razor was generally superseded by the safety razor.

The strops gave the Smiths an advantage over their competitors, in having two good selling lines. As strops sold in large quantities before the days of safety razors and the Smiths seem to have advertised theirs quite extensively, they probably formed the basis of what was to develop into their considerable export trade. Anyway, the early specialities of W. & A. Smith were Scottish hinged snuff boxes with lids painted or decorated with pen-and-ink work, and razor strops. Names of the well-known artists employed by the trade generally in decorating boxes and so on have already been given, so are not repeated here. The razor strops were always, and the Scottish hinged snuff boxes were generally, made of sycamore, but a range of expensive amboyna boxes was made by Smiths and other makers, and a few boxes were also made by various makers from particular oak, elm or other trees which had associations with famous people or buildings.

Sycamore, which grows to great perfection in Scotland, was an ideal wood for snuff boxes and other small woodware, such as strops. When first cut, it has a clear, white appearance, which turns creamy or yellow with age and exposure; it seasons well, is devoid of unpleasant smell or taste, is very mild and free from warping, and reasonably free from knots. It works easily and to a smooth finish and is particularly suited as a background for the paintings or pen-and-ink drawings, which were applied to early boxes, such as the interesting table snuff box, Plate 38, which is dated 1823. Fitted with the famous close fitting wood hinges, with half the knuckles cut into the back of the box and half into the lid, this box, known as the Solway box, is 4 in. long $2\frac{1}{2}$ in. wide and $1\frac{5}{8}$ in. deep, has rounded corners and is lined with lead foil. It is an outstanding and particularly well-finished specimen, decorated with neatly set-out black ink drawings on all six faces of the natural polished sycamore ground and appears to have been made regardless of expense, for a presentation. The story links Scotland, England and the Isle of Man and, like so many objects of its period, it also does homage to Robert Burns. The lid of the box depicts Robert Burns, framed in an oval which is inscribed at the top 'The Ayrshire Bard', and at the base 'Nat. 25 Jany 1756. OB. 23 July 1796'. The oval is set against an attractive and well-drawn background of thistle leaves and flowers; below, is a strip of landscape showing, on the left, the cottage where Burns was born, and on the right, Alloway Kirk and graveyard. On the base of the box is an illustration of the Burns Mausoleum, inscribed 'Mausoleum Dumfries. Founded 5 June 1815. Building cost L.500. Bust L.700'. Below this is Robert Burns' facsimile signature.

The story of the Maryport/Newcastle canal project is told by pen-and-ink drawings which run round the sides of the box. The front is divided into three zones. The centre one is inscribed 'To James Holmes Esqr from J. Grierson', above the three-legged Arms of Man and the date 1823. The side zones are occupied by maps of the two extreme ends of the proposed waterway. On the left is inscribed the British Ocean (no North Sea apology about it!), where the canal emerges at Shields. On the right is Solway Firth, showing Maryport and Allonby. The connection between these two ends of the canal is delineated on the back and ends of the box. The centre portion of the canal, below the hinged back of the box, gives a scale in miles, and proclaims 'Plan of the proposed Canal between Newcastle and Maryport is intended for vessels of 60 Tons—Cost about L300,000. Annual revenue is estimated at L30,000 Sterling'. The drawing of the canal shows all place names and geographical features along the route and makes it clear that it was intended to follow closely the line of Hadrian's Wall. The canal is shown as running nearly parallel to the coast from Maryport to Allonby, opposite which it crosses to the north side of the wall, continuing until it meets another canal, then recently opened, which ran from Port Carlisle to Carlisle. Approaching Carlisle, the joint canal is shown as cutting south through Hadrian's Wall, looping south of the city and continuing south of the wall until after passing Brampton, when it loops north again. At Haltwhistle it comes south of the wall and then closely follows the northern bank of the Tyne, entering it at Newcastle.

It may be assumed that James Grierson, the donor of this fascinating snuff box gift, was trying to persuade James Holmes to back the canal scheme. James Holmes, who lived another thirty years after he received the snuff box, was, with his brothers Henry and John, a partner in the Douglas and Isle of Man Bank, which their father founded in the late eighteenth century.

Additional to their bank partnership, the three brothers were engaged in the island herring fishery and fish curing; they were also ship owners and merchants, with extensive property interests both in the Isle of Man and in England. The family is believed to have been of Liverpool origin, and when they died, they were interred there in Low Hill Cemetry. No information seems available regarding James Grierson, but members of the Grierson family were living in Maryport in 1829.

A canal project from Solway Firth to the British Ocean was first planned in 1795; the canal between Carlisle and Port Carlisle was built between 1819 and 1823. It was not a paying proposition and about 1853 it was converted into a railway. In 1821, a Mr. Chapman reported on the alternative costs of continuing the canal from Carlisle to Newcastle, or building a railway between the two places. His estimate of £888,000 for the canal and £252,000 for the railway, won the day for the railway. The difference between Chapman's and Grierson's estimates for the canal may also explain why Holmes apparently did not support the canal project. Unfortunately, neither the artist who decorated this box nor the maker's names are known. For other good quality, hand-decorated boxes which do show makers' names, see the captions to colour Plates 30 and 31 and Plates 35 to 37.

The razor strop, Plate 42, bears the arms of William IV, from whom W. & A. Smith received the Royal Warrant in 1832. These strops are very early examples of transfer work, and, unlike the later work which was varnished, are beautifully french polished. Smith's name, the royal coat of arms and the wording INIMITABLE STRAP are all executed by transfer and it was probably the simplicity and satisfactory nature of the transfer application on these strops that eventually led the Smiths to launch their range of souvenir pictorial transfer ware. Certainly it was the gift to us of this strop from Mr. Mitchell of Sea Traders, Glasgow, in 1957, which first led us to associate the Smiths of Mauchline with the transfer ware souvenirs of views in all parts of the United Kingdom.

Birmingham

In 1829, the Smith business had reached such a size that the brothers opened a warehouse and showroom in Birmingham; a little later, they added a Birmingham factory for certain complete articles, some components and

ANDREW SMITH,

(Of the late Firm of W. & A. Smith,)

MANUFACTURER OF

SCOTCH SNUFF BOXES,

ETC. ETC. ETC.

To His Late Majesty.

MANUFACTORY, MAUCHLINE, AYRSHIRE.
WAREHOUSE, 139, GREAT CHARLES STREET,
BIRMINGHAM.

AGENTS. { MR. S. WARD, LOWTHER ARCADE, LONDON,
{ MESSRS. DELAVAL BROTHERS, PARIS.

LADIES' WORK BOXES; CIGAR MAGAZINES AND TEA CADDIES;
CIGAR, CARD, TOOTHPICK, AND SPECTACLE CASES;
TABLE AND POCKET SNUFF BOXES,

With a variety of other FANCY ARTICLES, all finished in styles peculiar to this branch of Manufacture; or made to order, with particular Subjects, Views, Coats of Arms, and Crests, correctly and beautifully painted.

TESTIMONIALS
Regarding the Mauchline Snuff-Box Manufactory.

TO THE MOST NOBLE THE MARQUIS OF HASTINGS, &c.

Windsor Castle, 5th July, 1832.

My DEAR LORD,—I have not delayed to submit your Lordship's letter of the 1st instant to the King, who has honoured me with his commands to assure you that His Majesty has great pleasure in complying with the application made through you by W. & A. Smith, Manufacturers of Snuff Boxes at Mauchline, in Ayrshire, that they may be permitted to style themselves Manufacturers to His Majesty. The King was much interested by your account of them.

Believe me to be, my dear Lord,

Your Lordship's very obedient and faithful Servant,

(Signed)　　　H. TAYLOR.

In Mr. Andrew Smith, who presents this Address, I recognise one whose elegant and unrivalled manufacture is spread over all countries.—*Lord Eglinton's Reply to the Address of the Inhabitants of Mauchline*, 8th March, 1841.

We set off in a post-chaise to Mauchline, fourteen miles on the Dumfries road, there to see the native place of Robert Burns, and to see also the most ingenious, the most interesting manufacture of snuff-boxes made of the wood of the sycamore, and painted and finished in all the various shapes and colours that the manufacture exhibits to the eye. Mr. Andrew Smith, one of the proprietors, most obligingly conducted us through the several departments. Some of the workpeople were hewing out the wood, which, from that rough state, we saw passing on from hand to hand, till it became an elegant piece of furniture for the pocket. Some were making drawings upon paper; others making the printings upon boxes; and all was so clean and so neat, and every person appearing to be so well off.—*Cobbett's Northern Tour.*

MAUCHLINE BOX MANUFACTORY.—A visit to this repository of taste, where mechanical ingenuity and artistical talent are pre-eminently conspicuous, is productive of the highest gratification.——*Kilmarnock Journal.*

No stranger passing through the small, though neat, yet unbusiness-like village of Mauchline could possibly dream of such a branch of industry being carried on so extensively within its boundaries. The visiter is completely taken by surprise. He may have heard, perhaps, that very beautiful boxes are manufactured by Mr. Andrew Smith, but his fancy must come far short of the endless variety of articles, of the most exquisite workmanship, which he finds displayed on entering the ware room.——*Ayr Observer.*

Fig. 4. Andrew Smith's Birmingham advertisement of 1843.

[95]

SCOTCH SNUFF BOXES.

WILLIAM SMITH,
MANUFACTURER OF
SCOTCH SNUFF BOXES
To His Late Majesty.

◆

WAREHOUSE, 27, BENNETT'S HILL, BIRMINGHAM.
MANUFACTORY,
MAUCHLINE, AYRSHIRE, SCOTLAND,
AGENCY—46, LISLE STREET, LEICESTER SQUARE, LONDON.

◆

CIGAR, CARD, AND NEEDLE CASES,
INKSTANDS,
TEA CADDIES, LADIES WORK BOXES, &c.

MAKER OF
THE INIMITABLE RAZOR STROPS.

WILLIAM SMITH, by his peculiar mode of producing patterns on the various articles of his manufacture " like silk woven in the loom," has (with his late partner) had the honour of executing the specimens of the different Clan Tartans for The VESTIARIUM SCOTICUM, published by Tait, Edinburgh, of which a Review of that Work speaks as follows:—" Many of these tartans are truly beautiful; though no doubt they may owe part of their splendour to the artist or illuminator. But the style in which they are executed, and their dazzling effect, must be seen to be comprehended. We do not pretend to describe by words either the process of painting them or to give any idea of the brilliant results. * * * * * The illustrations, the ILLUMINATIONS, the TARTANS, are the novel feature of the work; and without the actual vivid representations of these beautiful and delicate fabrics be seen, glowing in all the colours of the rainbow, no adequate idea of the work can be formed. * * * * All must give place to the rich, glowing, and resplendent specimens of the several tartans.

W. S. has always on hand at his warehouse, **27, BENNETTS HILL,** a large assortment of **SCOTCH SNUFF BOXES, &c.** in great variety of design, and also in the style above described.

ORDERS EXECUTED TO ANY PARTICULAR PATTERN.

Fig. 5. William Smith's Birmingham advertisement of 1843.

[96]

SCOTCH SNUFF BOXES.

ANDREW SMITH,

MANUFACTURER OF

SCOTCH SNUFF BOXES, &c.

TO HIS LATE MAJESTY,

MANUFACTORY, MAUCHLINE AYRSHIRE,

WAREHOUSE, 139, GREAT CHARLES STREET, BIRMINGHAM,

AGENTS.—MESSRS. DELAVAL AND MARESQUELLE, PARIS.

WORK BOXES, CIGAR MAGAZINES,

TEA CADDIES, NEEDLE BOOKS,

SOUVENIRS, CIGAR, CARD, TOOTHPICK, AND SPECTACLE CASES,

WAX TAPER, LIP SALVE, COLD CREAM, & TOOTH POWDER BOXES,

With a variety of other Articles, finished in styles, peculiar to this branch of Manufacture, or made to order, with particular Subjects, Views, Coats of Arms, and Crests, correctly and beautifully painted.

MANUFACTURER OF THE

INIMITABLE RAZOR STROP,

AND OF THE

SCOTCH OR AYRSHIRE HONES.

Breadalbane Buttons.

UNDER THE ESPECIAL PATRONAGE OF H. R. H. PRINCE ALBERT.

A. S. Inventor of the Breadalbane or Scotch Wood Button, begs to intimate to the trade that he commences the Season with a great variety of new Patterns, and with a stock which will ensure the prompt supply of their orders.

This Button gives entire satisfaction in the durability of wear and firmness of shank, while for lightness, beauty and variety of ornament it exceeds anything that has been made.

Fig. 6. Andrew Smith's Birmingham advertisement of 1847.

for finishing processes of some of their wide range of goods, which extended to papier mâché and metal. In 1829, they advertised in the *Birmingham Directory*:

'Smith, W. & A. Snuff box manufacturers and dealers in water Ayr and Scotch hones, powder of hone, razor strops, etc. 42 Hall Street and Mauchline, Ayrshire.'

The Birmingham business prospered and in 1833 they moved to 62 Constitution Hill. In 1835, they moved to 28 Great Hampton Street. By 1842 they had, additionally, premises at 27 Bennett's Hill. On the dissolution of the partnership in 1843, William (I) kept on the Bennett's Hill premises and took a warehouse at 56 New Street, whilst Andrew moved to 139 Great Charles Street. In that year, and again in 1847, they advertised individually in the Birmingham trade directory—see Figs. 4, 5, 6 and 7, which give a good idea of the range of their goods and the scope of their trading. Andrew's 1843

THE BREADALBANE
BUTTON, SCOTCH SNUFF BOXES, &c.

WILLIAM SMITH,

(MANUFACTURER TO HIS LATE MAJESTY,)

WAREHOUSE, 56, NEW STREET, BIRMINGHAM.

MANUFACTORY, MAUCHLINE, AYRSHIRE.

Cigar, Card, Razor, Lancet, Spectacle, Toothpick

AND NEEDLE CASES,

SOUVENIRS, INKSTANDS, LADIES WORK BOXES, &c. &c.

All in the beautiful and peculiar style of

THE SCOTCH SNUFF BOXES.

Fig. 7. William Smith's Birmingham advertisement of 1847.

advertisement, Fig. 4, confirms that the partners received the Royal Warrant from William IV in 1832. It will be noted that in 1843, William claimed to be the maker of the Inimitable Razor Strops, but in 1847 it was Andrew who made the claim. In 1846, the year before his death, William Smith was advertising again from 28 Great Hampton Street, as well as at 56 New Street.

As mentioned earlier, after the death of William (I), Andrew revived the title of W. & A. Smith, with his son William (II) as partner. W. & A. Smith continued to trade in Birmingham until 1904, occupying various premises, the last twelve years at 25 Mary Ann Street.

Inventiveness of the Smiths

It is interesting to see, from the changing trade entries and advertisements of the Smiths, how live they were—always abreast of, or ahead of the times in offering new and attractive lines and finishes and, as we shall show later, always inventing new machines, registering new designs, and seeking to improve the quality, output and value of their products. Of the two brothers, William, who is said to have been an art student in Paris and Brussels, seems to have been the artist, and Andrew the inventor, but both appear to have been good businessmen, with plenty of drive. William (II) seems to have been both inventive and clever at design.

The individual advertisements of 1843 and 1847 repay careful study. Although the brothers had greatly increased their range of goods and had added 'cigar magazines' (cheroot cases) to compensate for the fall off in snuff box sales, both still advertised the snuff boxes and, in turn, the razor strops which had originally brought them fame. Both now had agents in London; Andrew also had French agents, Delaval and Maresquelle of Paris. By 1847, both were advertising the Breadalbane wood buttons, which had soft shanks and were to be an important part of Andrew's business for many years to come, and Andrew states that he was the inventor. In 1843, Andrew, although making tartan ware, was still concentrating his advertising on hand-painted woodware. William was advertising both papier mâché trays and the new clan tartans. It is interesting that in the 1843 advertisement, Fig. 5, William refers to having (with his late partner). . . 'had the honour of executing the specimens of the different clan tartans for *The Vestiarium Scoticum* published by Tait, Edinburgh . . . '. This reference to the book already published, precedes by seven years the 1850 publication of a similar nature, which several other writers have noted and which was described as '. . . executed by the machine painting process introduced by the Messrs. Smith for their tartan woodwork and for beauty of execution and exactness of detail have not been excelled by any method of colour printing subsequently invented'. This may well be true, but William (II) invented, in November 1853, a new machine which greatly speeded up the established ruling, or checking machine, as it was more generally called. This new machine—'Patent 2639—Improvements in Ruling Ornamental Figures'— was a brilliant multiple-pen ruling device, which would have done justice, in the clean cut of its design and ingenuity, to 1953. Space will not permit of its full description here, but briefly it permitted a number of 'repeats' to be delineated simultaneously and, if required, in different colours. The machine, set with 16 pens, is shown in Fig. 8. In 1856, William (II) amended the machine so that small wheels or rollers took the place of pens. Oil or varnish colours could be used too, on this further improved machine, instead of the water colours which hitherto had been employed, and then sealed and finished by several subsequent coats of varnish. This latest machine was also intended for use on leather cloth, in addition to paper or direct wood decoration. From 1835, the Smiths produced fine quality tartan boxes, each with a portrait of Bonnie Prince Charlie inside the lid.

It has been stated that the earliest Scottish wood hinged snuff boxes were those decorated with the imitation niello or 'Scoto-Russian' scrolled designs and that this soon went out of fashion. Both these statements are incorrect. This design was probably first produced in 1842 or 1843; it was shown at the Great Exhibition of 1851, where W. & A. Smith won a gold medal for this work. It imitated Russian niello by covering the exterior of wooden boxes, etc., with heavy tin or gold foil, which was painted and then engraved so that the silver or gold colour showed through. In 1861, the success of the line prompted the inventive William (II) to devise yet another supplement to his Patent 2639, this time for replacing the pens with cutting points and adapting the machine to make '. . . either straight or waved lines producing ornamental figures upon metallic or other surfaces . . .'. The inventor designates this type of ornamenting 'Scoto-Damascene Work'. Very little of the Scoto-Russian niello and the Scoto-Damascene work has survived, probably because the metal foil peeled off.

[100]

Lord David Stuart had interviews with the late Mr. William Smith (William III), aged 73, in 1936 and was able to obtain some first-hand information from him. He also purchased some hand-painted Smith snuff boxes and, perhaps, most important of all, the Smith album of patterns, compilation of which may have been commenced some 120 years earlier. The album is a weighty tome, measuring $17\frac{1}{2}$ in. by 12 in. by 2 in. Although

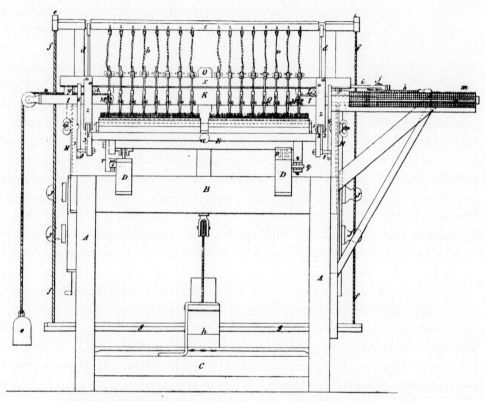

Fig. 8. Blueprint of Smith's ruling machine, Patent 2639.

many of the pages are blank, it contains 55 pages of coloured patterns of chequers, lines and other all-over designs, totalling 795 coloured patterns. Four of the patterns from one of the pages of tartans are shown in colour Plate 33. Additionally, there are $1\frac{1}{2}$ pages of Gothic and Classical designs in black and white (60 in number), one page of Classical figures in grey and white (12 in number) and $6\frac{1}{2}$ pages of engravings (87 in number) of well-known pictures, including sporting, landscape, historical, religious, townscape, seascape, theatrical, Burns and Wilkie subjects, etc., some of which were used for copying as hand-painted and pen-and-ink work pictures on the early snuff boxes.

The Smith Correspondence

We now come to a series of letters, which we possess, written by the Smith family between 1841 and 1846. Although charred by the fire which, in 1933, destroyed the 'Boxworks', as it was called by the people of Mauchline, these letters, in spite of their tantalizing gaps caused by the burning, still provide much fresh and fascinating detail of the Smiths and their business. Andrew seems to have visited London on business quite often during these years. The first letter was a personal and affectionate one from him in London, to his wife, Nanny, in Mauchline. Its only interest is that it is dated May 1840, and bears the new 1*d.* black stamp. A letter dated March 24, 1841, to him at the Smith's London agency, 49 Lisle Street, Leicester Square, from A. Young (his manager?) at Mauchline, tells of the rather rushed dispatch of the sample 'Queen's Box'. This was evidently a new line with the picture of Queen Victoria on the lid, as shown in Plate 34, and Andrew doubtless wanted to show it to his London agents. It was a success and was made for many years. Other boxes had heads on them, particularly Bonnie Prince Charlie's. The same letter gives details of orders for, and dispatch of tartan cigar magazines, some with vignettes on them, tartan razor strops and cases, and tartan door plates. There is also a reference to a new machine invented by Andrew and the letter ends with the information that 'Master William (William (II), then aged 14) gets on with the drawing of the acanthus—family all well— work people behaving very well'.

The tartan door or finger plates, made in sets with tartan door knobs, a speciality of the Smiths, were made of sycamore and were beautifully finished with tooled gilt bevelled edges and concealed slot screwed fixings. Two specimens are shown in Plate 41.

By March 1843, we find William (II), aged 16, living in Birmingham, probably with his sister Jane, working by day and studying at night under W. C. T. Dobson at the Birmingham School of Design. He writes to Andrew at Mauchline—'I am doing the Discobulus at the School of Design. I believe the Fighting Gladiator is to be the Prize figure . . . I am overrun with orders for small buttons, do let me have some soon.' There is also a reference to the firm's amboyna boxes (mentioned several times in the correspondence), which were one of their expensive specialities, made throughout the five years of the correspondence, and to showing a customer some inkstands.

Then follow, in February and March 1843, three letters from Jane in Birmingham to her father, Andrew, in Mauchline. They refer to orders for Memorandum Books (bottom left Plate 32), Ladies' Companions (right of Plate 40), the new Scoto-Russian boxes—sold out and urgently needed, tartan razor handles and a new line, tartan ear-rings and brooches (top, left of centre, colour Plate 32), which Jane had not yet seen. She also urges Queen's Head boxes for London orders, refers to the arrival of Delavel fans from Paris (so the business was two ways), and further refers to orders galore for buttons. A postscript to her letter adds 'I had a letter from Willie this morning, he is in great spirits both about his drawing and orders'. So Willie (II), aged 16, was evidently getting around, but where was he? Perhaps studying and working in London or Paris. After 1843, no correspondence of Jane's seems to have survived, but by January 1845, Willie, then aged 18, was back in Birmingham and, judging by the correspondence, was running the by no means inconsiderable business there. The tartan button business was booming —'orders galore'. Willie was very pleased at getting back old customers who had left them earlier, through delays in executing orders. On September 24, 1845, Willie writes to his father full details of process and cost and diagram for a new stoving oven which he is proposing to install, for speeding up the finishing of buttons, both of wood and iron. One of the varieties, but we cannot tell which, cost $2\frac{1}{2}d.$ per gross.

Two days later, Willie wrote again to his father at Mauchline. He refers to making his own dies for box lids, instead of buying them from outside and reckons that the 'plate slips' will in future cost '4/-$d.$ to 4/6$d.$ per doz., instead of 14/- to 20/-$d.$ paid to Davis'. This presumably refers to transfer work, now coming increasingly into the picture. The boxes decorated by this process are always described in the correspondence as common boxes. The Scoto-Russian range was, however, still selling well, and tartan razor strops, spectacle cases and match stands or boxes were in demand. Much of the correspondence is taken up with complaints regarding overcharges for delivery by railway and steamboat, about which Willie became very annoyed. Times do not change! The value of goods dispatched from Birmingham in

Fig. 9. Smith's transfer plate of Eastbourne views.

September, 1845, was £334 18s. 0d., and this seems to have been a fair average, so at that time the turnover from the Midlands branch was about £4,000 per annum.

In a postscript to a letter which Willie sent his father in October 1845, he refers to an American customer wanting his buttons with cloth shanks in future and goes on '. . . he says he believes it will soon be the same in this country—so you were not far wrong when you said that you thought the cloth eye would be preferred'. Willie then goes on to describe the practical difficulties of fixing cloth shanks to wood buttons and how he thinks they can be overcome. The difficulties were overcome and the first enthusiast for the cloth shanked button in Scotland was the Marquis of Breadalbane, after whom the buttons were named. They were made of sycamore and decorated, in three price ranges, with pen-and-ink work, tartans and transfers.

Thanks to Lord Bute, we are able to include here a letter written in 1842 by Earl De La Warr to the 2nd Marquess of Bute. It concerns an order for six snuff boxes selected by Queen Victoria from samples submitted by the Smiths of Mauchline.

Buckhurst Park,
December 31, 1842.

Dear Lord Bute,

The best apology I can make to Mr. Smith (and I am well aware that I owe Him one) will perhaps be the announcement to Him that the Queen has graciously selected two or three articles out of the lot which Mr S first submitted for inspection—and has commanded me to order for Her six snuff Boxes of the largest size shewn—with the full Royal arms upon the lid. But now comes the strange part of my story. In all the hurry and bustle of the London Season—and particularly at the moment of Mr. Smith's application (the period of the Fancy Ball) I put away the things which the Queen did not take in so safe a place that I cannot find them. However I have no doubt that—on my return to London—they will be forthcoming. At the same time I wrote a letter to Mr. Smith—which I now perceive from your note He did not receive— and which I have no doubt is with the missing articles. In the mean time however Mr S. might put his order in hand and may make Himself easy about the other things for which I of course make myself responsible.

[105]

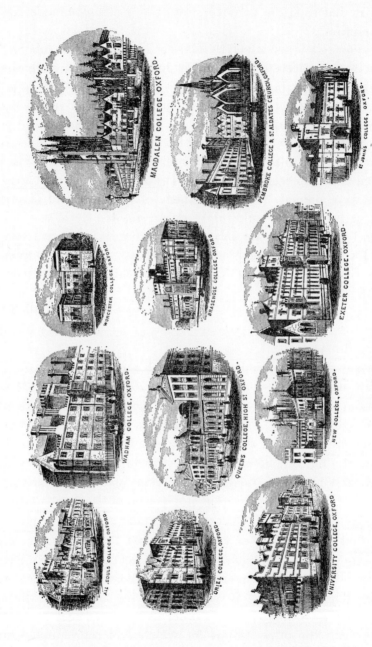

Fig. 10. Smith's transfer plate of Oxford Colleges.

Mr Smith did not leave his address when last He called at my House, and I do assure you I was on the point of writing to you on the subject when your note arrived.

Pray Believe me
dear Lord Bute
always yours most sincerely
De La Warr.

Tartan Ware

The tartan ware first produced by various Scottish makers in the 1820s was painted direct on the wood, but it could not have been long before the Smiths, the largest makers of tartan ware, began their mechanizing of the process and the painting of the tartan on paper, which they glued to the wood. So perfectly was this done, however, and so good the glue, that even with a powerful magnifying glass, it is most difficult to tell today which process was used. Some of the paper joints, such as the compound curves which arose on crook parasol handles and on the tapering holders of pens, must have been extremely difficult to make so neatly. Examination shows that the procedure adopted was to paint the wood black where the junction of the tartan would occur; then, if there were any gap in the tartan joint, it did not show against black, as it would have done against the natural sycamore. Sometimes joints were marked by a wavy, gold, tooled line. Edges of boxes, penwipers, cheroot cases, etc., were similarly treated with black paint before the paper was applied. On most of the Smith tartan ware, the name of the clan tartan was printed or transferred in gold lettering. In Plate 40 is shown an attractive calendar which Smiths designed, in the 1840s, for the French market, the lady's companion, referred to in the correspondence, a book or blotter cover, with a picture coloured by one of Willie's patented processes, a parasol handle, a spectacle case and a pencil. Tartan ware seems to have been made by Smiths at least to the end of the nineteenth century, but the later examples are not as good as the earlier ones.

Transfer Ware

The earliest example of the transfer ware which we have seen is the razor strop, with Royal Arms of William IV, which was made between 1832 and

[107]

Fig. 11. Smith's transfer plate of views in London and Boulogne.

1837, Plate 42. The really large flow of transfer ware, such as the selection shown in Plate 44, apparently dates from about 1845, although the pen-and-ink and hand-painted ware still continued, but with diminishing sales. Judging by transfer pictures which can be dated, the zenith was between 1860 and 1900, but the Smiths probably continued to make it on a diminishing scale, until the 1933 fire. Transfer ware obviously commenced as an attempt to simulate pen-and-ink, hand-drawn or wash pictures which, with rising labour rates, were steadily becoming more expensive, in a world which was clamouring continuously for ever cheaper souvenirs. We use the word *world* deliberately, because the Smiths' trade in souvenir ware, although it doubtless commenced with Scottish scenes and Burns associations, did indeed become world-wide. Before transfer ware came to an end, it was itself imitated by the sticking on of photographic labels, both black and sepia, which were varnished over. Where these souvenirs were made and by whom, we have been unable to ascertain.

For many years, we thought that most of the English scene transfer ware must have been made somewhere in England, and for some years we endeavoured to find out where. We followed up many clues of names printed on the bases of boxes and other novelties, but found them all to be booksellers, fancy goods or stationers' shops, or other local retailers of the souvenir ware. However, examination of thousands of English scene transfer ware products and comparison with similar objects decorated with Scottish scenes convinced us that all the actual woodware concerned came from Scottish manufactories, even if the decoration were applied by various firms in different countries.

Eventually, luck came our way: we found that the original Smith engraved copper (early) and steel (later) plates for the various transfer engravings of scenes had survived the 1933 fire and we were able to purchase a wide selection of them. These plates are in excellent condition, as shown by the election of non-Scottish engravings, Figs. 9 to 16, taken from some of them. The plates were made by F. Pritty of Birmingham and other engravers in London, Sheffield, and elsewhere. The transfers were made by the Smiths themselves, on a machine which they kept in the varnish room of the boxworks.

We had thus now ascertained that the Smiths not only made the woodware, but also applied the transfer pictures of scenes, public buildings and hotels in London, Oxford, Cambridge, Stratford-on-Avon, Windsor, and all the other

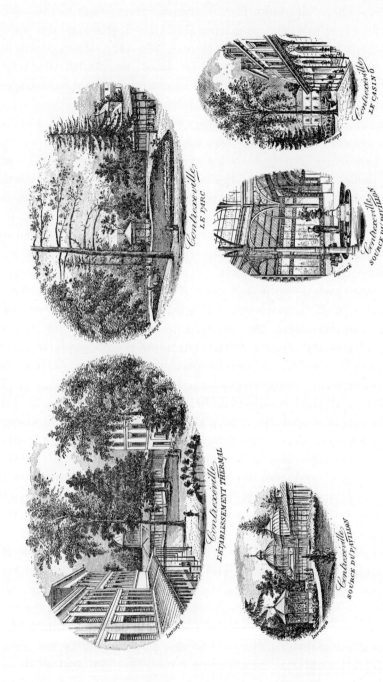

Fig. 12. Smith's transfer plate of Contrexeville views.

popular tourist centres and seaside resorts and their piers, in England and Wales, as well as a vast range of views in Scotland, including very small places. They also did the same for the United States, Australia, India and countries on the continent of Europe.

Each plate which we purchased is packaged in a paper wrapper, transfer printed with the several scenes engraved on the plate and numbered serially.

The method of transferring was, first, to coat the box with two or three coats of shellac and the face of the print was also varnished. The print was then put ink side downwards on the object being decorated, and left to dry, which took one to two hours. The print was then sponged and the Japanese paper was rubbed off with a damp cloth.

At this stage in our investigations, there occurred a fantastic coincidence, which enabled us to check that nearly all these plates really were used by one firm, the Smiths of Mauchline. One summer's afternoon in 1959, the inter-com rang in our first-floor lounge and our receptionist told us that old friends of ours, Mr. and Mrs. Manheim from London and Miss Manheim from New York, were downstairs viewing the Pinto Collection of Wooden Bygones. We went down and chatted to them and were introduced to their friend, Mr. Timothy Trace, the antiquarian bookseller from Peekshill, New York, who had come with them. We invited them up to tea and Mr. Trace noticed the Smith transfer engraving plates which had just arrived and were spread out on a table for examination. They excited him because he said he was sure that he had an album containing the same engravings and he offered to send it over from America for us to see. He did so and he had made no mistake: he had one of the Smiths' traveller's albums. Amongst the groups of engravings in the album were some which contained the same selection of views and were numbered the same as some of the wrappers and engraving plates which we had. Plate 43 shows the exterior of the album, entitled *Views for Sycamore Work*, and the index pages of the album form Appendix II. This particular album probably represents the territory of one traveller—the south and west of England, Wales, the Midlands and north-west England. Probably another traveller, with another album of views, covered the east and north-east of England, together with Scotland, and doubtless there were further albums for the continent of Europe, and for America, Australia and India. What an amazing coincidence it was that the one man who could complete our evidence should come from New York and arrive in our lounge

Fig. 13. Smith's transfer plate of views in Cannes and Nice.

at the precise moment of one day in 1959 when the plates were laid out there.

We do not want to give the impression that the Smiths of Mauchline were the only makers of transfer ware—they were not; but they were probably first and they were certainly the last in the field and they had far and away the largest range and selling organization. The extent of the opposition which they met in transfer ware is almost impossible to gauge, because few specimens are stamped or imprinted with makers' names. The Smiths themselves only seem to have put their names on their strops and on advertising novelties; vendors' names are fairly common. Mr. John Buist, a collector of transfer ware, has given us details of a transfer ware tea caddy and a transfer ware cigar case imprinted with the name of Davidson, Wilson & Amphlet, who were competitors of the Smiths in Mauchline. We have a snuff box with a coloured transfer picture of good quality, which is imprinted by W. Johnston of Auchinleck.

One way and another, the summer of 1959 was a great breakthrough for us in our research on Scottish ware. We had two articles published in *The Scotsman* in August and September 1959, entitled *The Enterprising Smiths of Mauchline*. These articles brought us a lot of correspondence and interesting information. Most important of all, from our point of view, was that they put Lord David Stuart in touch with us. At that time, Lord David had been collecting information for more than twenty years, with a view to writing a book on Scottish woodware. After he had read our two articles, he wrote to us suggesting that we should write a monograph and, with unparalleled generosity, offered to place at our disposal all his notes and papers, to augment our own. This Scottish section, therefore, represents the combined research of Lord David Stuart and ourselves, further augmented by those others whose names are included in the acknowledgments.

Whether the Smiths sold all their French transfer souvenirs through their Paris agents or through agents in various towns, we know not; but we have the engraving plates (some of which are reproduced in this chapter) of scenes in Paris, Boulogne, Calais, Cannes, Nice and Contrexeville—all, be it noted, places popular with British tourits, who would doubtless buy the already familiar transfer ware and bring it back again to the British Isles! One reciprocal result of the Scottish woodworkers' success on the continent was that it led to continental manufacturers invading the English market

Fig. 14. Smith's transfer plate of various French views.

with a range of very passable imitations of the Smiths' work. In the Pinto Collection, Birmingham Museum, is a bodkin case with a view of Horse Guards Parade, London, marked 'Manufactured abroad' and we have a record of a view of 'The Old Chain Pier, Brighton' on a box marked 'Made in Germany'; we have also heard of Japanese imitations.

We have already mentioned that the Smiths had a sale for buttons in the United States, so it may have been through the same customer that they sold their transfer ware range, with views of Washington, Niagara, and other places—for some of the American views depicted, see Fig. 15.

From the files of the *Ayr Advertiser* we have a good clue, too, as to how the enterprising Smiths came to sell their range of woodware with views of Sydney (see Fig. 16) and Melbourne, Australia, for in 1858, there occurred a Smith social function which has a bearing on this. It appears that in January 1858, the Smith family and a few of their friends were entertained to supper by workmen in the newly erected shop of the firm; the company numbered 160. It sounds as if the firm were very prosperous and that there was an excellent family atmosphere between employers and employees, particularly as, in the same month, Andrew's daughter received from the work people in the boxworks a valuable silver teapot, on the occasion of her marriage to a Mr. Muir and of her departure for Melbourne—hence the Australian contact. Incidentally, Mrs. Muir (née Smith) had a daughter who returned to Ayr and lived to be 93.

It looks as if a regular annual Hogmanay celebration took place, for a year earlier the work people had held a soirée at which Andrew had spoken and said that Mauchline owed much of its notoriety to the genius of Burns, whose wife came from a family which had lived in the village from time immemorial. At the time of this soirée, little more than 100 years ago, there were four contemporaries of Burns still living in Mauchline—three men and a woman, whose ages ranged from 82 to 90.* The three men attended the soirée, but the woman, Helen Miller, was prevented by infirmity from doing so. She had known Burns well and had been a domestic servant with a family named Waddle in Mauchline, with whom Burns' younger brother, William,

---

* Mauchline must be a healthy place, for we have received, directly and indirectly, considerable information from other 'youthful' folk in this district, who come in this same age group!

Fig. 15. Smith's transfer plate of American views.

was an apprentice saddle-maker. One of the three men was a servant lad at Mossgiel Farm, Mauchline, when the Burns family was there.

A photograph of Andrew, with a grandson, Plate 48, taken in 1865, four years before his death, has an inscription on the back, reading:

'Andrew Smith aged 69. Commenced working with his own hands and alone, to make wooden snuff boxes in Mauchline in the year 1821. This occupation now gives employment and a comfortable subsistence to more than 400 men, women and youths.'

It is difficult to be sure whether this large total of hands applied to the firm and its sub-contractors or the whole of the Ayrshire souvenir industry, but there is probably not much difference, because the Smiths had more or less wiped out all opposition by 1865, which was probably their peak.

The Beginning of the End

By 1900 the business had shrunk sadly. We have a photograph taken in 1900, against the exterior of the boxworks; it shows three men, eighteen women and a boy. One of the men was probably Robin Kirkland, who worked the transfer printing machine in the varnish room at that time.

The third William Smith, now aged 37, had suffered many blows. Pen-and-ink work and Scoto-Russian niello were dead. Sales of the still well-made woodware, but in a deteriorated tartan finish, were dying, and even transfer ware sales, for long the mainstay of the business, were shrinking, due to foreign competition. An attempt had been made, we believe, to boost sales with a range of advertising novelties imitating lacquer and papier mâché— floral designs on a black or cream lacquered ground; these were probably a product of the 1870–80 period. They do not seem to have had much success, for here again competition was cut-throat from completely mechanized products. There was also a loss of customers due to amalgamations. This particularly applied to the principal Scottish thread firms who, when they were all separate organizations, vied with one another in the presentation of their threads in attractively designed tartan and transfer ware boxes and miniature barrels made by the Smiths.

The last William (William III) tried to revive the fortunes of his old-

Fig. 16. Smith's transfer plate of views in Sydney, Australia.

established firm with yet another decorative finish, fern ware, decorated with ferns from the Isle of Arran. Although, judging by survivals, the project had some success, sales could never have attained the volume of the earlier forms of decoration. The ferns were collected every summer from Arran by a Mr. Andrew Miller, who was a relative of Helen Miller, already mentioned; Andrew Miller lived in Mauchline and Smith sent to him, at his house, the various wooden souvenirs to be decorated. This work went on between 1900 and the late twenties. Like all the earlier forms of decoration, it commenced as a hand process, but ended up with transfer pictures of fern arrangements and, alternatively, photographic labels. The last were sometimes superimposed on a tartan background, as photographs of actresses and other celebrities, and scenes associated with Burns were also used.

The fern decoration process practised by Miller was kept very secret and still remains somewhat of a mystery. It seems to have commenced as a laborious method of arranging and sticking actual ferns on a wood or paper-covered wood background, and then varnishing over. The work done by this process is easily distinguished from other processes by the raised ferns. Later, there developed a process which involved a lady assistant of Miller's, who pinned down the actual ferns on to the bare wood, with hundreds of small pins, and dusted over with some kind of talc powder. The ferns were then treated as a reverse stencil and the background between them then seems to have been spattered with some very thick, treacly brown pigment; the ferns were next removed, the pin holes stopped and the markings of the ferns carefully painted or stained in, after which the whole object was varnished. Objects treated in this manner show the light coloured ferns as depressions in the brown background. The cheapest process imitated the last by covering the keepsakes with paper printed in close simulation of the last described process. The paper-covered woodware can be distinguished by the smooth, single plane surface of fern and background; careful inspection discloses the joints in the paper. Examples of the fern processes are shown in Plate 45.

After the fire of 1933, the boxworks turned, as a last resort, to making whitewood boxes for amateurs to decorate, and they also made larger objects, such as wheelbarrows. At the beginning of 1937, William Smith (III), still a bachelor, retired; his employees were ageing, no young recruits were coming in, and demand was dying anyway, so it is not surprising that the outbreak of World War II finally brought this fine old firm to an end.

PART THREE

BOIS DURCI

Bois Durci

IT MAY SEEM peculiar to include a plastic in a book written about decorative woodware, but *Bois Durci*—the literal translation is hardened wood—is a wood-based plastic of considerable merit, both artistic and useful. Indeed, it can claim to be the father of modern plastics, having antedated celluloid by one year. Celluloid, originally known as Parkesine and now called Xylonite, was first made by Parkes of Birmingham in 1856. It was used essentially for utilitarian objects and had the disadvantage of inflammability.

Bois Durci was non-inflammable, very hard and strong, and it could be moulded to a very high finish, so that it served the purpose of providing fine and almost indestructible ornament or ornamental objects at a small fraction of the cost of making them by hand in wood or other materials. The inventor was Monsieur Charles Lepage of Paris, who described himself as a literary man; he took out provisional patents in France and England in 1855. The actual manufacturer of the product was a Monsieur Latry of Paris. The English patent, No. 2232, dated 5th October, 1855 was for a composition of materials intended as a substitute for wood, bone, rubber, metal and other hard or plastic substances, particularly where the same were manufactured into useful and ornamental objects. According to the details given in the specification, it consisted, in the main, of a combination of sawdust (said to be chiefly rosewood and ebony sawdust) and albumen. If desired, the sawdust could be mixed with vegetable or mineral colouring matter or metallic powders and the albumen with any glutinous substances; alternatively, the sawdust could be combined with other glutinous or gelatinous substances, such as gelatine or size, or with albuminous salts. The inventor, however, preferred pure albumen from eggs, blood, etc. The process employed for the manufacture was to soak the sawdust, with or without other powders, in pure albumen, slightly diluted with water. The mixture was then dried, placed in a steel mould of the required shape and subjected to pressure in a hydraulic or other suitable press. While undergoing pressure, heat was simultaneously applied to the mould by a steam jacket, hot plates, surrounding it with hot bars, by direct or radiated heat, or other suitable means. As soon as the moulding was completed, the mould was cooled by immersing it in cold water, or by pouring cold water over it. The method of manufacture sounds, and the press (Fig. 17) looks, remarkably modern for an ornamental plastic, made 115 years ago, and certainly the resultant product was as good as anything we can turn out today.

It was claimed additionally that metal castings or ornaments in relief, in metal or other material, could be applied on the composition before pressure, or the articles could be ornamented by engraving the inner surface of the moulds in which they were shaped. All these claims are fully substantiated by *Bois Durci* products which are still extant and some of which are illustrated here.

The inventor particularly recommended his material for knife handles, pipes, dominoes, chessmen, picture frames, boxes, cornices, furniture, combs, box covers, brooches and other articles of jewellery. The majority of these objects were certainly made in *Bois Durci*, but the greatest number of survivals are from a series of circular ornamental plaques, $4\frac{1}{2}$ in. in diameter, with backgrounds $\frac{1}{4}$ in. to $\frac{5}{16}$ in. thick, on which are raised relief impressions, mainly of European royalties or notabilities of the third quarter of the nineteenth century, and also of religious subjects. A few of these plaques are a rather dull and muddy bronze colour, but the majority are jet black and doubtless this was a considerable attraction in an age which esteemed carved jet and the fine black basalt ware of Wedgwood.

The interesting and highly artistic series of *Bois Durci* historical plaques, examples from which are shown in Plates 50 to 52, will stand very favourable comparison with the finest Wedgwood modelling and there is no doubt that Lepage or Latry, in addition to possessing a good commercial flair for

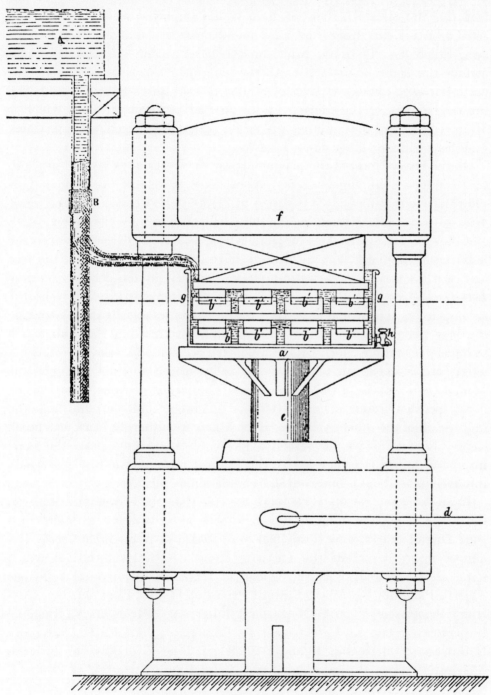

Fig. 17. Lepage's press of 1855.

[125]

featuring the particular 'lion' of the day, also employed an extremely gifted artist or artists, but apart from a commemorative medal of the 1862 Exhibition, which has 'T. Ganu, Sculᴰ' on the face, we have seen none which include the name of the artist. All the genuine *Bois Durci* plaques in this particular series, however, are signed with a small raised wing, placed below the cut off neck of the subject, on the matted background. This, which is composed of small dots, frames the relief, which itself resembles a polished, grainless ebony, or other dense hardwood.

On the back of most of the plaques appear the words BOIS DURCI in plain, raised letters, $\frac{1}{4}$ in. high, usually accompanied by one of the curious signs shown above the words BOIS DURCI, in Plate 51, H. Occasionally the words BOIS DURCI appear without one of these signs; the plaques of Cobden, 50, B, and Pius IX, 50, K, are cases in point, whilst Auber, 51, G, has not even the lettering on the back, but all of them have the wing modelled on the face and, as it is a part of the main impression, they can be considered as genuine *Bois Durci*. One would have imagined that the words BOIS DURCI and the accompanying sign would have been impressed automatically on the back by the base plate; there are, however, grounds for thinking that this was a secondary operation which could be omitted accidentally, because often the letters are crooked, out of alignment, badly spaced and not arranged the same on two replicas of the same subject. The plaque of Auber is one of the dirty, speckled brown or bronze-coloured specimens and the relief lacks the high polish of the other examples, all of which are either jet black or a much clearer brown. As we have seen a glossy black example from the same impress of Auber, our guess is that this particular plaque was 'under-cooked', intended to be a reject, but went into circulation by mistake.

In an era when royalty were more the rule than the exception in Europe, the range of popular subjects was very wide and, doubtless to maintain a good flow of orders, new heads had to be added at frequent intervals. Examples recorded include the following inscribed royal subjects, of which some are illustrated: 'Victoria, Queen of England', Plate 50, E.; 'Prince Albert', Plate 50, F; 'Albert Edward Prince of Wales', Plate 50, D; 'Alexandra Princess of Wales'; 'Napoleon I Empereur', Plate 52, A; 'Eugénie Impératrice', Plate 52, B; 'Napoleon III Empereur', Plate 52, C; 'Alexandre II Empereur' (of Russia), Plate 52, H; 'Franz Josef I' (of Austria); 'Charles XV' (of Norway); 'Vittorio Emanuele II' (of Italy), Plate 52, D; 'Isabel 2

Reina de las Espanas', Plate 52, G; 'Leopold I Roi des Belges', Plate 52, J; 'Napoleon Prince Imperial Né le 16 Mars 1856', Plate 52, E. It is interesting that Plate 52, F., is a bronze medallion of Napoleon identical with the *Bois Durci* example, Plate 52, C; this does suggest that a bronze master plaque was made of each subject.

Religious subjects include Jesus Christ, Plate 50, M, the Virgin Mary, Plate 50, L and Pope Pius IX, Plate 50, K. Among the notabilities commemorated were Wellington; Richard Cobden, Plate 50, B; John Bright, Plate 50, C; Viscount Palmerston, Plate 50, A; Schiller, Plate 50, J; Shakespeare, Plate 50, H; Lord Byron, Plate 50, G; Garibaldi, Plate 51, M; Wagner; Beethoven; Cavour; Auber, Plate 51, G; Abd-El-Kader, Plate 51, L; de Béranger, Plate 51, K; Molière, Plate 51, J.

Some of the *Bois Durci* medallions of Queen Victoria and Prince Albert are dated 1851, which may puzzle collectors; it does not mean, however, that they were made before 1855, the date of the patent; they are obviously copied from medals struck to commemorate the 1851 Exhibition. Doubtless the astute M. Latry produced each new plaque when the various personages depicted were at the height of their fame or popularity and, judging by comparison of *Bois Durci* plaques with other dated reliefs or portraits of the same subjects, the heyday of this outstandingly fine and artistic production was between 1855 and 1875. That it was dead before 1887 seems certain, otherwise there would be *Bois Durci* souvenir plaques of Queen Victoria's golden jubilee. Why the product fell out of favour and became a lost art will probably never be known now, but its strictly limited period of manufacture adds to its attraction as a suitable and profitable subject for the discriminating collector of the best Victoriana. A *Bois Durci* collection has the advantage that it takes up little wall space, is highly decorative, requires no attention, is not easily damaged and is still within reach of a modest purse, although it is steadily appreciating in value.

Monsieur Latry showed *Bois Durci* at the 1862 London International Exhibition and won medals in Class 36, 'Dressing Cases and Handbags, etc.' and also in Class 4, Section 'Vegetable Substances Used in Manufacture'. The *Bois Durci*, 6 in. diameter, commemorative medallion of the Exhibition is illustrated in Plate 51, E; it has the name of the sculptor, T. Ganu, bottom left above the border. In the Paris Universal Exhibition of 1867, Monsieur Latry's exhibits included a tazza, an oval box and cover and a small looking glass frame.

Bois Durci black medallions, rosettes and paterae were used extensively in France to reduce the cost of ornamenting the ebony cabinets in vogue; medallions depicting musical subjects, such as Plate 51, F, were inserted in the fronts of upright pianos. It is by no means certain, however, that all these medallions of musical, allegorical, or classical subjects are genuine *Bois Durci*: most of them bear no lettering on the backs, nor wing on the face and the dies do not always give the sharp impression and smooth lustre of the genuine article.

The $4\frac{1}{2}$-in. diameter *Bois Durci* series of notabilities was also made in smaller diameter plaques, for insertion into box lids and earlier royalties, including Queen Anne, were featured.

In addition to the undoubtedly genuine *Bois Durci*, there has also survived a number of very similar French and English plastics of the same period, made in both black and bronze colours. Some of them reach quite a high standard of excellence, but mostly they are better in execution than in design. They include circular snuff boxes, some of which are difficult to distinguish from wood, and a good selection of ornamental book-type frames for daguerreotypes, which were popular during the *Bois Durci* period. Three examples of frames are shown in Plate 52, K, L, and M, K, with a relief (of Cellini?) in a wavy border, is bronze colour; the others give the polished ebony effect. They are cleanly and sharply moulded and inside one leaf there is an engraved gilt mount behind glass, held by a gilt metal moulding; the opposite leaf is lined with a wine colour, embossed velvet pad. It is difficult to tell whether these are the genuine *Bois Durci* or not, and the same remark applies to the book-type pocket match box, Plate 52, N.

In the applications cited in Lepage's patent, moulded handles are included and reference is also made to the applying of relief ornament in metal to the plastic composition before pressure. The very charming lady in Plate 51, D, illustrated in detail in Plate 49, who was probably intended for an umbrella or parasol handle, shows effective application of silver inlay to the dark bronze plastic; the excellent quality of the modelling suggests that it is genuine *Bois Durci*, even though unmarked. Silver is used for the finely detailed ornament in the hair, for the ear-rings and for the necklace and pendant. In Plate 51, A, B and C, are shown some of the applications to jewellery, of *Bois Durci* and the like.

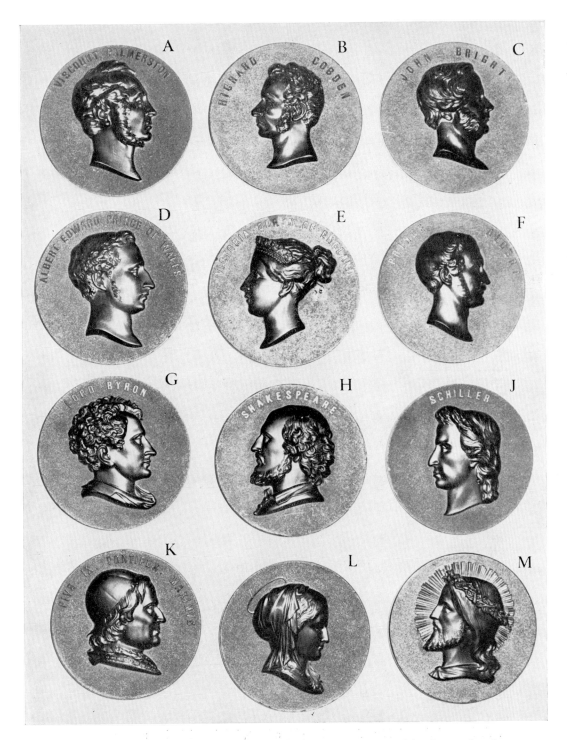

50. The fine quality and high artistic level of *Bois Durci* is shown in these medallions of **A**, Viscount Palmerston; **B**, Richard Cobden; **C**, John Bright; **D**, Albert Edward Prince of Wales; **E**, Queen Victoria; **F**, Prince Albert; **G**, Lord Byron; **H**, Shakespeare; **J**, Schiller; **K**, Pope Pius IX; **L**, the Virgin Mary; **M**, Jesus Christ. *Pinto Collection, Birmingham Museum.*

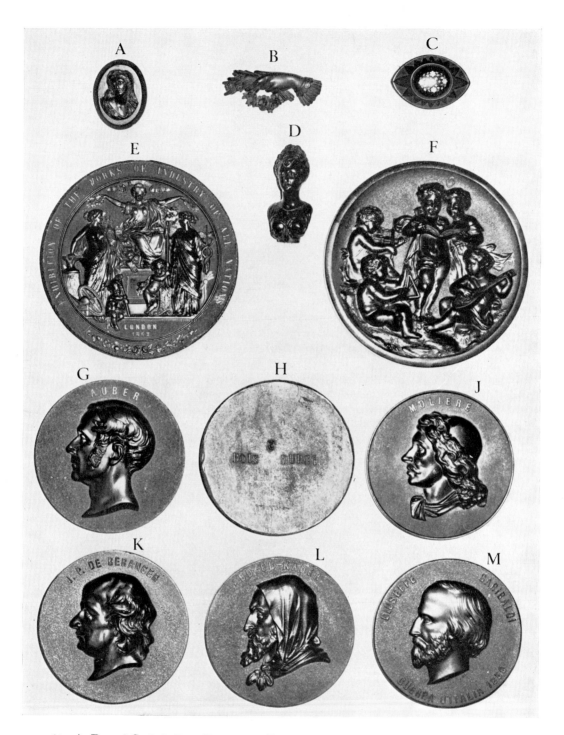

51. **A**, **B**, and **C**, *Bois Durci* brooches; **D**, a bust, inlaid with silver (shown in more detail in Plate 49); **E**, the commemorative medallion of the 1862 International Exhibition; **F**, plaque of the type used as ornamental inserts on upright pianos; **G**, Auber; **H**, markings on the back of a genuine *Bois Durci* medallion; **J**, Molière; **K**, de Beranger; **L**, Abd-El-Kader; **M**, Garabaldi. *Pinto Collection, Birmingham Museum.*

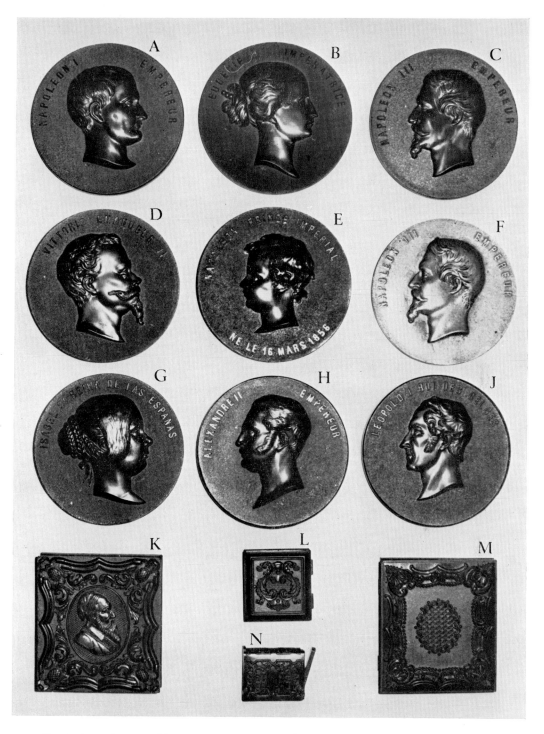

52. **A**, Napoleon I; **B**, Empress Eugenie; **C**, Emperor Napoleon III; **D**, King Victor Emanuel II; **E**, Napoleon Prince Imperial; **F**, bronze master medallion of **C**; **G**, Isabel Queen of Spain; **H**, Emperor Alexandre II; **J**, Leopold King of the Belgians; **K**, **L**, and **M**, three book-type daguerrotype frames and a pocket match box **N** of *Bois Durci* or similar type plastic. *Pinto Collection, Birmingham Museum.*

55. A very fine pyrographic panel, one of a pair, of a Russian market scene by Comte de Rottermund. The burnt lines are as fine as in an engraving. *Pinto Collection, Birmingham Museum.*

54. Asiatic battle scene, one of a pair, by Comte de Rottermund. Unlike most pyrographers, he used figured wood. In these panels, he shows its potentialities for sky effects. *Pinto Collection, Birmingham Museum.*

55. Ralph Marshall was a most versatile pyrographer. This is his self-portrait, executed by pyrography in 1835. *Pinto Collection, Birmingham Museum.*

56. For biblical scenes, Marshall developed a mystical misty light and shade technique, shown here in 'St Paul Preaching at Athens', dated 1836. *Pinto Collection, Birmingham Museum.*

57. Marshall's version of the 'Blinding of Elymas'. Note the range of expressions portrayed and the mastery of line. *Pinto Collection, Birmingham Museum.*

58. Marshall was very clever at obtaining candle and lantern light effects, rather in the style of Wright of Derby. This panel, dated 1834, is actually from a painting by Henry Morland. *Pinto Collection, Birmingham Museum.*

59. Another panel by Marshall, dated 1834; a lantern light effect, also copied from a Henry Morland painting. *Pinto Collection, Birmingham Museum.*

60. Joseph Smith seems to have specialized in pyrographic versions of well-known portraits. This is his copy of Hoppner's painting of the second Earl of Camden in Garter Robes. Date 1810. *Pinto Collection, Birmingham Museum.*

61. Panel of a girl praying, by the pyrographer signing himself E. H. G. His high lighting by the blow-lamp and gouge method and economy of lines were striking. *Pinto Collection, Birmingham Museum.*

62. The fox surveys the dead rabbit in the spring-trap; another work by E. H. G.
Pinto Collection, Birmingham Museum.

63. 'Waiting for the Plough' by I. W. Wells. Nov. 1, 1866. *Pinto Collection,
Birmingham Museum.*

PART FOUR

NINETEENTH-CENTURY PYROGRAPHY

Nineteenth-Century Pyrography

PYROGRAPHY, literally writing in fire, denotes poker work. Pyrography sounds, and was doubtless intended to sound, vastly superior to poker work. To many people poker work conjures up a vision of the utilitarian branding of ownership marks on carts, barrows, tool handles and the hidden parts of furniture, and lettering and figures on packing cases. To others, the depths of poker work are reached by crude 'decorative' plaques, with proverbs burnt on them, or announcements such as 'My Doggie' in burnt outlines, filled with crude colours and having a hook below for the dog lead.

The descriptions above are not of pyrography as our ancestors understood the term: to them, pyrography was an artistic craft—one of the oldest and most geographically widespread means of wood decoration. In Europe, it enjoyed a considerable vogue in the early seventeenth century and was used largely for the skilful decoration of small woodware, such as standing cups, which had clear lettering and outlines of birds, beasts, flowers and insects in intricate borders, similar in style to the work found on silver and in needle-work, of the late Elizabethan and James I periods. Later in the seventeenth century, furniture decorated with pyrographic perspective panels enjoyed a limited vogue in nearly all Western European countries, although some of the actual work was imported from the East. Pyrography probably attained its highest artistic standard in the nineteenth century, when the craft was mainly practised as a leisure hobby by amateurs, some of them highly gifted; it is doubtful, however, if many of their subjects were original compositions.

Apart from being a fashionable pastime for the amateur in the nineteenth century, the best pyrography of the period could never have been produced commercially, because the fine and intricate work would never have obtained a price commensurate with the time spent on it. It was doubtless, too, the slowness of the technique, requiring a skilful and detailed drawing on the wood before the hot-point lines could be incised, which led to so much pyrography being a translation of portraits and noted pictures into terms of burnt wood panels.

In *Memoirs of a Highland Lady*, the autobiography of Elizabeth Grant of Rothiemurchus, 1797–1830, the author writes about her uncle, Dr. James Griffith, who was head of University College, Oxford (1810–11):

'Through this library was a small room with a fireplace used by my uncle to heat his irons for his poker-painting . . . His graver style, whether in water-colours, chalks, reeds or burnt in, are considered to have shown great genius . . . The altar-piece in his own College chapel—Christ blessing the Bread—was of his own poker-painting. In the museum was a head, I think of Leicester, and while we were with him he was busy with a tiger the size of life, the colouring of the old oak panel and the various tints burnt on it so perfectly suiting the tiger's skin. Jane (younger sister of Elizabeth Grant) was his great assistant in this work, heating the irons for him in the little end room, and often burning portions of the picture herself.'

A panel of a tiger, but considerably less than life size, is in the Pinto Collection, Birmingham Museum.

In pure pyrography, no pigments were used and the monochrome pictures were obtained by burning the surface of a light coloured and usually rather featureless hardwood to varying depths, giving a palette from light brown, through sepia, to black. In one specialized technique, burning was combined with shallow gouging, to heighten effects.

The wood used had to be satin smooth and reasonably close grained, otherwise the burning ran along the wood fibres and ruined the picture; but even with all precautions, the work required considerable skill, because of the variable heat of all hot-points, prior to the comparatively recent introduction of controlled heating, of which the electric poker machine is the most complete. With this, the heat is continuous, and controlled either at a constant temperature, or variable at will. In earlier times, pyrography was executed by means of steel points, heated in a portable charcoal stove of pot form. Circling the pot, some 2 in. from the top, was a series of holes in which the pointed skewers, or pokers, were inserted for heating. The pokers, shaped rather like round files, provided with terminals of varying sections and sharpness, usually had handles of bound asbestos yarn. In the last quarter of the nineteenth century, gas and electric furnaces were introduced, with pokers having platinum points. These helped to reduce the bugbear of variable heat. All the panels illustrated here are too early for their executants to have been able to take advantage of this trouble-saver.

Additional to the poker, some pyrographers used blow pipes, by means of which it was possible to produce by burning all the effects, such as wash or tint, which are found in monochrome painting. The apparatus was rather like a scent spray, with a rubber bellows and tubing, which was used to blow ignited gas, petroleum, or spirit, from a bottle, through a flexible tube, into a metal point. A full account of the technique was given in *A Handbook of Pyrography* by Mrs. M. Maude (1891). It was a good practical treatise, although largely an advertisement for the 'Vulcan' Burnt Wood Etching Machine, made by Abbott Bros. of Southall. The Vulcan machine created tint or wash effects by means of heat from benzoline, regulated by bellows and tubing passing to a selection of platinum points, of which the various types are illustrated in the handbook. According to the book, the most commonly used woods for pyrography were sycamore, lime, holly, American white wood, chestnut, teak, aspen poplar, tulip, and the wood from Assam tea chests. The first three woods mentioned are the most recommended and our own research bears out that they were the most popular. Several teachers of pyrography advertised at the end of the book, including a Madame Korvin-Pogosky, who had won a silver medal for her work at the Edinburgh International Exhibition of 1890. Advertisers who supplied everything for the pyrographic artist, included William Whiteley, and Shoolbred & Co.

To obtain fine lines of light on a dark ground, surface scraping was employed and the aids of sepia and vitriol were not disdained by some pyrographers, for obtaining wide surfaces of brown or black.

A pyrographer who eschewed all artificial aids and produced the most finely detailed, purely burnt pictures, was the Comte de Rottermund. All that we have been able to ascertain is that he worked in Brussels early in the nineteenth century; we would be grateful for any further information about him. In the Pinto Collection are four large panels by him; one from each pair are shown in Plates 53 and 54. The lines on these remarkable pictures, so intricate in their details, are as fine and closely packed as in any etching, and there are no burn runs in the hatching, in spite of the difficulty of heat control at that time. Both pairs of panels suggest Russian backgrounds, the war themes appearing to be more Asiatic in their costume than the peasant scenes. We do not know whether these compositions are original or not, but groupings, movement, expressions and delineation are masterly, and the leisurely tempo of the peasant market scenes is conveyed just as vividly as the violence, action and carnage of the battle in the Asiatic scenes.

There are two minor mysteries about de Rottermund's work. Unlike other pyrographers, who worked mostly in the rather plain woods already listed, he used figured wood and took advantage of the natural mottle to obtain cloud effects. We cannot identify this wood; it has characteristics both of figured birch and satinwood, but does not appear to be either. It is from a very large tree, for each of these panels is an unjointed $20\frac{1}{4}$ in. wide. The second curious point is that these panels, which are all signed 'Cte de Rottermund', have at other points on the panels 'WR' and a series of Roman numerals, respectively CXXII, CXXIII, CXXIV and CXXV. Surely this king of fine pyrography could not possibly have had an output prodigious enough for these numerals to represent the panel numbers. It is interesting that, in each panel, de Rottermund shows the same predilection for a white horse in the foreground, which characterized the work of the seventeenth-century painter Philips Wouverman.

Now we come to Ralph Marshall, whose fine self-portrait in pyrography is the subject of Plate 55. It is dated 1835, so he must have been almost a contemporary of de Rottermund and an extremely gifted and versatile pyrographer. In the Pinto Collection are six panels by Marshall, all signed and all executed between 1834 and 1842. Nevertheless, he must have still been alive at least until 1851, for we also acquired the medal which was awarded to him for his pyrographic exhibits in the Great Exhibition of 1851. In several of his early works he portrays striking candlelight pictures which immediately call to mind the technique of Wright of Derby; the compositions and themes used, however, are not by Wright, but by Henry Morland, father of the more famous George Morland. Marshall's candlelight pictures are an astonishingly brilliant and successful use of pyrography. Two of them, Plates 58 and 59, both dated 1834, tell their own stories in striking terms of light and shade. The oil paintings from which these are taken were also translated into terms of glass pictures and of etchings.

Marshall executed some romantic pictures on medieval themes, not wholly successfully, and also some fine and intricate biblical pictures. These last he treated in a misty, mystical manner and introduced considerable use of gouge and blow-lamp. It appears probable that Marshall used both sepia and vitriol, to some degree, in all his compositions. The biblical scenes are copies of Raphael's tapestry cartoons in the Victoria and Albert Museum; one example, 'St. Paul Preaching at Athens', which is dated 1836, is shown in Plate 56 and another, 'The Blinding of Elymas', in Plate 57. In both, there is an extraordinary amount of detail and feeling of mysticism.

A much mistier panel, by an unknown pyrographer, which will not illustrate clearly, is a copy of Sir Joshua Reynolds' painting of 'The Fortune Tellers', which is at Blenheim. The gouge and blow-lamp technique is particularly apt for heightening the air of mystery of such a theme and it can be used, as it is in this example, to make the picture 'come and go', according to whether you are just to left or right of it.

A pyrographer who specialized in copies of full-length portraits of the nobility, was Joseph Smith. His skilful pyrographic version of Hoppner's portrait of John Jeffreys, second Earl of Camden, in Garter Robes, Plate 60, is dated 1810.

A good artist in pyrography, who high-lighted his work by the blow-lamp and gouge technique, signed his work with the initials E. H. G., but unfortunately included no date. Two examples of his work, Plates 61 and 62, show considerable skill and praiseworthy restraint in knowing when to leave off. The top right-hand corner of the panel, Plate 61, a girl praying, has been extensively damaged by worm. The fox surveying the rabbit in the spring trap, Plate 62, is one of a pair.

The $9\frac{1}{2}$ in. by $6\frac{1}{2}$ in. sycamore panel, Plate 63, is a straightforward and competent example of hot-point pyrography supplemented by judicious use of a narrow gouge. It is hot-point lettered on the back 'Waiting for the Plough' —'Burnt by I. W. Wells, Nov. 1, 1866'.

A nineteenth-century pyrographic artist whose work we have not seen was the Rev. William Calvert, Minor Canon of St. Paul's, who is said to have used ordinary pokers to execute an alterpiece 'Paul and Silas' in Cambridge University; he also made pyrographic pictures of scenes from Shakespeare.

Pyrography happily is not dead; it has practitioners today and among the most experienced and skilful are Mr. and Mrs. Peter Child, of The Old Hyde, Little Yeldham, Halstead, Essex, who wrote an excellent article on the subject in *The Woodworker*, October 1964.

It is a pity that so little information seems to be available about the practitioners of this craft—which was an art. We hope that its inclusion in this book may bring to light some details of the lives of the men and women who have left pyrographic mementoes of their skill and patience.

APPENDICES

South Coast Resort Stockists of Tunbridge Ware &/or Tunbridge Wood Mosaic

We are indebted to Mr. R. G. E. Sandbach, MA, Curator, Tunbridge Wells Museum, for the following list, which he has compiled.

Brighton

Chapman, Wm.	c. 1822	3 King's Road
Holding, Jas.	c. 1822	24 Little Castle Square
Hunt, John	c. 1822	Castle Square
Morris, Sarjeant Witton	c. 1822	27 Richmond Place
Murray, John	c. 1822	86 St. James' Street
Robinson, John	c. 1822	29 North Street
South, Frederick	c. 1822	33 Ship Street
White, —	c. 1822	St. James' Street
Bell, Elizabeth	c. 1822–4	3 King's Road
Fry, —	c. 1822–4	Cavendish Street
Morris, J.	c. 1822–4	27 Richmond Place
Upton, W.	c. 1822–4	Boyce's Street
Izard, John	c. 1822–40	18 St. James' Street

Arnold, Lucy (?)	*c.* 1839–40	118 London Road
Braddock, James	*c.* 1839–40	162 North Street
Buhrer, Joseph	*c.* 1839–40	28 North Street and 1 Ship Street
Chassereau, Susan	*c.* 1839–40	21 North Street
Childs, Wm.	*c.* 1839–40	53 King's Road
Clark, Samuel	*c.* 1839–40	In the market
Greenin & Co.	*c.* 1839–40	13 North Street
Irvin, —	*c.* 1839–40	Civet Cat, 111 St. James' Street
Jaquemart, A.	*c.* 1839–40	17 Old Steine
Melhuish, Elizabeth	*c.* 1839–40	63 Western Road
Morris, Christopher	*c.* 1839–40	Repository, Richmond Road and 79 King's Road
Morris, Edward	*c.* 1839–40	Richmond Gardens
Saunders, Edward	*c.* 1839–40	26 New Road
Smith, Mary Ann	*c.* 1839–40	64 West Street
Souch, Elizabeth and Mary Ann	*c.* 1839–40	52 North Street
Childs, Wm.	1845–73	Fancy Repository, 51 King's Road
Perry, R. H.	From 1873	Same address as above

Dover

Licence, R.	*c.* 1870	Marine Parade Library, 11 Marine Parade

Hastings

Morris, Edward	—	47 George Street
Woods, John	—	4 George Street

Rye

Green, Thomas Littleton	1931–9	Mosaic Works, Market Street

Weymouth

Medhurst, James	*c.* 1846–59 Ceased before 1875	Tunbridge Warehouse, Maiden Street and Tunbridge Ware Manufactory

Out of all the above, we only know definitely that Green and Medhurst were actually makers of the woodware. We think it is highly probable that the remainder were only stockists, although Sarjeant Witton Morris, John Izard, and W. Upton at Brighton are classified as Tunbridge Ware Manufacturers and Dealers, and Robert Licence at Dover as an Ivory and Hardwood Turner and Tunbridge Ware Manufacturer.

The preceding list is extracted from the few directories of the period which define trades; it does not mean, however, that the persons named were only active in these years.

Index of a Regional Book of
English Transfer Views

This book, with leather spine and leather corners, is a traveller's regional 'sample' book of W. & A. Smith of Mauchline, Ayrshire—see Part II, Chapter 4, page 111.

VIEWS FOR SYCAMORE WORK
Index
Page